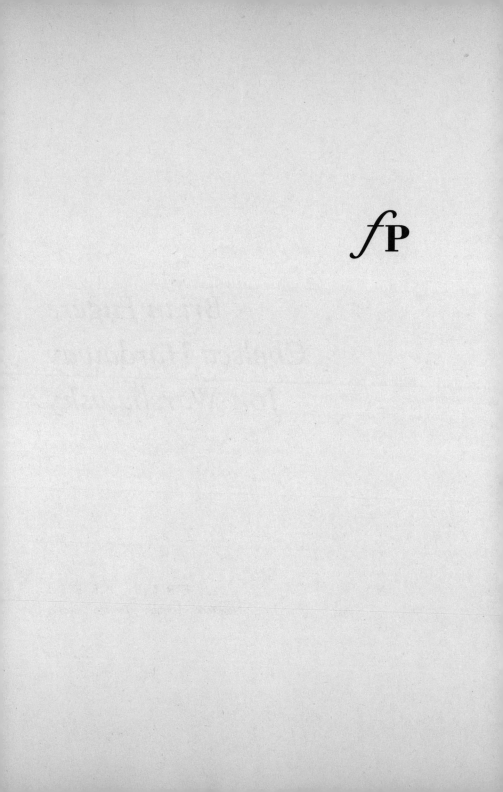

ƒP

Brian Fugere
Chelsea Hardaway
Jon Warshawsky

FREE PRESS
New York London Toronto Sydney

Why business people speak like *idiots*

A *bullfighter's* guide

*f*P

FREE PRESS
A Division of Simon & Schuster, Inc.
1230 Avenue of the Americas
New York, NY 10020

Designed by Karolina Harris

Manufactured in the United States of America

10 9 8 7 6 5 4 3 2 1

Library of Congress Cataloging-in-Publication Data
Control Number: 2004061967

ISBN 0-7432-6909-8

For information regarding special discounts for bulk purchases,
please contact Simon & Schuster Special Sales at 1-800-456-6798
or business@simonandschuster.com

Fondly dedicated to Lawrence Tureaud
(better known as Mr. T)

He said it best:
"Don't gimme none o' that jibba-jabba!"

CONTENTS

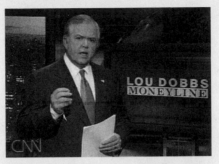

June 17, 2003 (transcript)
CNN Moneyline *with Lou Dobbs*

A new software program sends a clear message to corporate America—cut out the bull.

New York-based Deloitte Consulting admits it helped foster confusing, indecipherable words like "synergy," "paradigm," and "extensible repository," but now it has decided enough is enough. On Tuesday, the company released "Bullfighter" to help writers of business documents to avoid jargon and use clear language.

"We've had it with repurposeable, value-added knowledge capital and robust, leveregable mindshare," Deloitte Consulting partner Brian Fugere said.

THE LANGUAGE
OF BUSINESS

L et's face it: Business today is drowning in bullshit. We
try to impress (or confuse) investors with inflated letters
to shareholders. We punish customers with intrusive,
hype-filled, self-aggrandizing product literature. We send ele-
phantine progress reports to employees that shed less than
two watts of light on the big issues or hard truths.

The average white-collar worker goes to the office every
morning, plugs into e-mail, dials into voicemail, and walks
into meetings only to be deluged by hype and corporate-
speak:

> *After extensive analysis of the economic factors and trends
> facing our industry, we have concluded that a restructur-
> ing is essential to maintaining competitive position. A
> task force has been assembled to review the issues and
> opportunities, and they will report back with a work plan
> for implementing the mission-critical changes necessary to
> transform our company into a more agile, customer-
> focused enterprise.*

He sees right through it, too, because these contrived
communications are the exact opposite of the natural conversations he engages in everywhere else. Outside of work, he
has a fundamentally different kind of conversation—a human
one, with stories and color. Informal, spontaneous, warm,
funny, and real. Then he hops online, and the natural and un-
filtered dialogue continues in chat rooms, message boards,

blogs, and instant messaging. Even his virtual life is more real than his office life.

There is a gigantic disconnect between these real, authentic conversations and the artificial voice of business executives and managers at every level. Their messages lack humanity in a world that craves more of it. Between meetings, memos, and managers, we've lost the art of conversation. *Bull has become the language of business.*

But most business people stumble forward in a haze. They copy and paste and crank out hollow and vapid communications that become the butt of jokes as soon as they leave the e-mail server. Even worse, they get ignored. They're full of jargon, they say very little, and—most important—these messages are out of touch, arrogant, and condescending. And everyone knows this, except for the idiot hitting the Send button.

PERSUASION

We've become immune to these empty, generic messages. And as a result, no one really *listens* anymore.

Enough with the endless charts and graphs; enough with the templatized mission statements; enough with the pre-digested language. What's the compelling point? Why should I listen? Is anyone worried about what I'm worried about? Do they get it? Will the truth ever show up in my inbox? Don't hold your breath.

This is troubling, because almost any time we need to deliver a message at work, it's because we want to persuade someone to think or do something. We persuade people to hire us. Then we persuade them to approve our budgets, sponsor our projects, or buy what we're selling. If we're lucky, we'll also persuade people to do their assigned tasks, and persuade others to promote us.

When everyone tunes out, this persuasion doesn't happen.

Persuasion is so important. One 1995 study by Donald McCloskey concluded that one-quarter of the gross domestic product is linked to persuasion.*

So here's what you need to know: You have a huge opportunity to become more persuasive. To be that one infectious human voice—the one that's authentic and original and makes people want to listen. In a world of business idiots who can't make anyone care, this is your golden opportunity.

How can we have such confidence in you, having only met you a page ago? Well, we can't. You may be the poster child for mediocrity when it comes to writing or giving presentations. Or you may run the Microsoft grammar checker in Word and think, "This is brilliant, an incredible gift—I should accept every suggestion!"

But we're betting that you're like us.

We're betting that you want to be heard.

ORIGINS OF THE BULL SPECIES

So how did it get this bad?

There are many reasons, all of which ensure that nobody makes any real promises or delivers any real meaning. The tide of political correctness has stranded us so that business idiots can't speak frankly about anything. Fear of liability or even responsibility rules the day, and attorneys shape every document into a promise-free blob of text that deliberately says nothing. And then there are business schools, consultants, and gurus, all of whom make a living repackaging old concepts as something "new."

Beyond that, there's technology, which makes it all too

* Donald McCloskey and Arjo Klamer, *American Economic Review,* May 1995, Vol. 85, No. 2.

convenient to automate the one part of business that should *never* be outsourced: our voice. Whether it's using someone else's jargon, a generic template, or even a speechwriter, too many business people give away their biggest chip in the influence game without a thought. The temptation is everywhere. We now have the option of deleting our personality from what we say and write.

YOUR OWN FUZZBUSTER

Navigating our way through business communications is like driving on a Georgia highway—there are traps everywhere. What we need is our own business Fuzzbuster. If you want to connect with an audience, the traps are a roadmap to being heard: if you know them, you can avoid them.

At their root, the traps are about obscurity, anonymity, the hard sell, and tedium:

- **The Obscurity Trap.** *"This is just the kind of synergistic, customer-centric, upsell-driven, churn-reducing, outside the box, customizable, strategically tactical, best-of-breed, seamlessly integrated, multi-channel thought leadership that will help our clients track to true north. Let's fly this up the flagpole and see where the pushback is."* These are the empty calories of business communication. And, unfortunately, they're the rule. The Obscurity Trap catches idiots desperate to sound smart or prove their purpose, and lures them with message-killers like jargon, long-windedness, acronyms, and evasiveness. The ones who escape do so through plain language and candor.
- **The Anonymity Trap.** Businesses love clones—they're easy to hire, easy to manage, easy to train, easy to re-

place—and almost everyone is all too happy to oblige. We outsource our voice through templates, speechwriters, and e-mail, and cave in to conventions that aren't really even rules. What business idiots have forgotten is that your personality is the thing that helped you make friends, find a date, get a mate, and probably even get a job. It may take some work to create an original message, to make people smile, or to stop running your office life through your e-mail inbox, but if you want to escape the Anonymity Trap, that's where you have to start.

- **The Hard-Sell Trap.** Legions of business people fall prey to the Hard-Sell Trap. We overpromise. We accentuate the positive and pretend the negative doesn't exist—not because we received our business training on used-car lots, but because we're human, and we like to be optimistic. The result is that we do too much hard selling. This may work for those pushing Abdominizers on late-night television, hoping to sway a few clueless, lonely, or drunken souls. But it's dead wrong for persuading (sober) business people to listen. At the end of the day, people hate to be sold to, but they love to buy. With access to loads of information and instant communication, people today question everything. They know the hard sell and—with trust in business at an all-time low—even the slightest whiff of it sends people running for the exits.
- **The Tedium Trap.** Everyone you work with thinks about sex, tells stories, gets caught up in life's amazing details, and judges others by the way they look and act. We live to be entertained. We all learned that in Psychology 101, except for the business idiots who must have skipped that semester. They tattoo their long, executive-

sounding titles on their foreheads, dump prepackaged numbers on their audience, and virtually guarantee that we want nothing to do with them. Death by generalization replaces those spontaneous, personal, and compelling details. But if you have a good working knowledge of storytelling, conversation, procreation, and recreation, you can escape the Tedium Trap.

YOUR HUGE OPPORTUNITY

Great business leaders live life outside the four traps. Honest language; the hard truth; a passion for what they're doing; a personality that shows up at the office five, six, or seven days a week—we recognize these people, and we love to hear from them. Jack Welch, Warren Buffett, and Jeff Bezos have all found ways to make straight talk a hallmark of their companies, and any of them can fill an auditorium at will. Yeah, the CEO at our company knows widgets and gives speeches. But Virgin CEO Richard Branson is the business equivalent of a rock star.

Jeff Bezos built Amazon.com from a wobbly Internet startup to a viable business, and took a lot of punches from a cynical press. But every time we heard from him during those tough years, it was like listening to a boy who had just unwrapped a mountain of presents on Christmas morning. Bad earnings news was everywhere during the startup years, and Bezos owned up to every bit of it. No jargon, no excuses, no bull. Just a lot of zeal and a lot of personality at the office.

Entire careers can be built on straight talk—precisely because it is so rare.

This goes well beyond grammatical rules or fashionable expressions. It requires honesty, humanity, and confidence from business people. Anyone can put together a presentation that describes the "extensible synergies derived from repurposing intellectual assets." It takes more work to express the idea (no, we don't know what it is) in plain English.

We're not recommending that you go back to Rhetoric 101. And don't get the impression that this book was written by a bunch of grammar geeks waiting to spank you for using a gerund, unless you're into that. (Gerunds, we mean.) This book is about being yourself, reclaiming your voice, and letting some personality, warmth, and humor into your work life.

The payoff for this is huge, mostly because so few people are trying. The messages around you are so bad, you'll be surprised how far a little straight talk, humor, and storytelling will take you.

Beyond that, it's a lot more rewarding to bring your real voice to work. We may save ourselves some effort by using templates, burying our noses in e-mail all day, and sticking to the same stifling agenda all the time, but that's not what makes us happy outside of work. It's a fool's—that is, an idiot's—errand to think it's going to lead to nirvana in the cubicle.

There is a ton of mediocre books out there on bad business writing. However, there are no mediocre books that get beyond picking on grammar to throw some light on *why* and *how* the voice of business became so dull. That's about to change.

This is your wake-up call. Personality, humanity, and candor are being sucked out of the workplace. Let the wonks send their empty messages. Yours are going to connect.

I

The Obscurity Trap

I notice that you use plain, simple language, short words and brief sentences. That is the way to write English—it is the modern way and the best way. Stick to it; don't let fluff and flowers and verbosity creep in.

—Mark Twain

1

THE FOG OF BUSINESS

Enron's performance in 2000 was a success by any mea-
sure, as we continued to outdistance the competition and
solidify our leadership in each of our major businesses.
We have robust networks of strategic assets that we own
or have contractual access to, which give us greater flexi-
bility and speed to reliably deliver widespread logistical
solutions. . . . We have metamorphosed from an asset-
based pipeline and power generating company to a mar-
keting and logistics company whose biggest assets are its
well-established business approach and its innovative
people.

—ENRON ANNUAL REPORT, 2000

Unless a businessperson gets cornered into speaking directly to live people—say English teachers bearing as-
sault rifles—we know what to expect: an indigestible
main course of catchphrases and endless prose, with not a lot
of substance for dessert.

Jargon, wordiness, and *evasiveness* are the active ingredi-
ents of modern business-speak, and they make up the Obscu-

rity Trap. This trap is particularly pervasive, and its perpetrators are evil people who want to destroy civilization as we know it. (Well, okay, not really, but it felt good to get that out.) We call this a *trap* because the people who spew jargon and all of that evasiveness really aren't evil at all.

They're us.

In normal, healthy conversations with their friends, spouse, cat, and Porsche, these people are brilliant communicators. Ask them to give a presentation or write a press release, though, and say hello to Mr. Hyde. Out comes the 80-page presentation about "synergistic alliances" and "go-forward engagement processes." And all of this goes right the past the audience, so the lonely yet meaningful point on slide No. 78 doesn't have a chance of getting through.

And it isn't just a matter of spending more time and effort. Consider the press release. Almost nothing goes through more editing and review cycles than a press release, which has to be short and is written for the world at large. And yet, press releases seem to show that the more time that is spent on a message, the *worse* it gets. Shown (p. 13) is an excerpt from an IBM press release.

If you were to take a red marker and cross out the acronyms and meaningless jargon in this press release, the next person who walked by would probably call for an ambulance, because it would look as if you were bleeding all over the page. Once again, here's a smart and respected firm in technology services that can't break away from clichés or corporate-speak long enough to tell us anything understandable.

The Obscurity Trap is a serious problem for anyone who wants to connect with a reader or audience: nature has given us the ability to ignore all of this stuff, and we ignore it all the time. Just as you don't put much thought into walking or breathing, you dismiss the empty or contrived calories of

---

Hundreds of Business Application Software Providers Flock to IBM's Partner Programs
Growth Continues in Industry and SMB Markets

SOMERS, NY—July 19, 2004—IBM today announced that business application software providers worldwide are flocking to IBM's partner programs for vertical industries and small and medium business (SMB). The PartnerWorld Industry Networks, ISV Advantage for Industries, and ISV Advantage for SMB initiatives provide independent software vendors (ISVs) with the technical, marketing and sales resources and support to jointly capture industry-specific and SMB market opportunities worldwide.

More than 900 ISVs across 43 countries have joined PartnerWorld Industry Networks, a major initiative that is helping an expanding ecosystem of industry focused partners to more effectively work with IBM marketing and sales organizations to deliver customized solutions to customers. Covering the banking, financial markets, healthcare, life sciences, retail, telecommunications and recently announced government and insurance industries, PartnerWorld Industry Networks will continue to expand to support additional verticals, with prioritization based on ISV input . . .

---

modern business communications without disturbing many slumbering brain cells. And if you tune them out, you can bet your audience does, too.

THE ROOTS OF OBSCURITY

If the Obscurity Trap is all about jargon, wordiness, and evasive language, it's fair to ask why otherwise decent people feel the need to torture their colleagues. There are external forces—political correctness, risk management, and the herd mentality. But there are more insipid, internal factors at work as well.

ME, ME, AND—COME TO THINK OF IT—ME

The first reason for obscurity is a business idiot's *focus on himself over the reader*. In the IBM press release, jargon and acronyms serve the author, not the hapless reader who is supposed to get some meaning from it.

When obscurity pollutes someone's communications, it's often because the author's goal is to *impress* and not to *inform*. The low road to impressing an audience is to make them feel inferior, by using words they won't understand. So a fallback plan when trying to impress (or when you have nothing to say) is to toss in a few ringers like "value proposition," "mindshare," and "ecosystem." This way, the author seems to be a kind of intellectual powerhouse, generating concepts that are too lofty to be expressed in something as mundane as English. There's a strange insecurity at work here, where someone tries to overcompensate by trying to sound smart.

PERVASIVENESS OF EVASIVENESS

A second reason people fall into the Obscurity Trap, and ultimately speak like idiots, is a *fear of concrete language*.

In business, we like to avoid commitment. Liability scares us, so we add endless phrases to qualify our views on a topic, acknowledging everything from prevailing weather conditions, to the twelve reasons we can't make a decision now, to the reason we all agree the topic is important, to the reason why decisions in general require a lot of thought, and so on.

As a study in contrast, consider wedding vows, with the traditional "I do." Two short words, nowhere to hide. No qualifying clauses, no royal "we" to relieve individual accountability. Just *I* promising to *do*.

A lot of the Obscurity Trap stems from evasiveness. If you don't want to say anything, you'll find a way to say nothing in a lot of words. Readers will recognize this and give up looking for meaning.

ROMANCING THE DULL: MIAMI RECEIVABLES

The third motive for obscurity is business idiots' relentless *attempt to romanticize* whatever it is that they do for a living. All of this romanticizing keeps the business world from talking about work and instead allows business idiots to pretend to be secret agents and quarterbacks.

When it comes to careers, there are basically two kinds of people in the world. The first kind can mention their career at a cocktail party and count on being swarmed by people who want to know what it's really like. If you're an international spy, actor, or sports star, you have what doctorates in the career sciences call a "cool job."

For most of us, though, fame isn't part of the job description. We get e-mail, send e-mail, detach things from e-mail, save those things, read them, and make some edits. Sometimes we file them or make copies of them so we don't lose them. We share them with other people who change the format of these things and show them to groups of other people. We stow things away for a while. Then we retrieve them and take little parts of them and put them into bigger files, where they become part of what we call "intellectual capital" (because we don't want to call them "bigger files").

Our friend Avril Dell, a consultant based in Canada, put it bluntly: Business is dull, and that's why we've yet to see a television drama along the lines of "Miami Receivables." It isn't hard to see her point. We tried, though:

Palm trees sway in front of a sleek glass office building. A tan stud in a five-figure suit hands the Ferrari keys to the valet, sweeps into the office, winks at the supermodel who's temping as the receptionist between Sports Illustrated *swimsuit issue shoots, and brings up PowerPoint.*

He launches the auto-content wizard but then— boom—a window explodes (well, OK, bear with us) across his screen announcing that he has a new mail message. Decision time. Will he launch Outlook or continue selecting the color scheme for the presentation? Or get wild and dial into voicemail? Or decide the pressure is too much and head down to the lobby café?

No, it's voicemail. He swivels in his chair, suavely taps the speakerphone, and slides his finger over to the high-tech button that says VOICEMAIL. *After glancing to confirm his privacy Steve Studly taps in his secret access code. A tired voice comes over the speaker: "Forwarding." Then a bored voice: "Forwarding." Weary monotone: "Forwarding on behalf of Jim Deevers." Then a stern, official-sounding "firm communications." Then an imperious "Jim Deevers."*

The suspense builds, and at last Jim Deevers drops the bombshell: "On behalf of the entire executive committee and other senior people whose photos you may have seen in our annual report, I'm pleased to report that our United Way campaign is 4 percent ahead of last year." (Commercial break here.)

Even the most skilled screenwriters, none of whom had anything to do with the preceding, would have a hard time selling a drama based on the daily routine of the average businessperson. This insecurity is another reason business people become business idiots. We all want to be stars. So the roots of business idiocy—the disastrous communications from guys like Jim Deevers—have a lot to do with the psychology of making business sound cool.

Before you raise the white flag and sell your soul to the idiots, consider how avoiding the Obscurity Trap and doing away with jargon, wordiness, and evasiveness can make you a star. Put your audience first, and inform them instead of trying to impress them; make a strong, specific commitment instead of resorting to the usual business vagaries; and embrace what you do instead of trying to romanticize it.

THE STARBUCKS STUDY

By now you're probably wondering if this is really worth it. Obscurity is everywhere, and it takes real effort to avoid it. Does it really matter?

We decided to put it to the test. In August 2003, we chose an Atlanta Starbucks to study the effect obscurity has on people. The approach was simple: We showed a bunch of everyday people one of two actual company writing samples. One was straight and clear, the other was typical corporate speak—full of bull (in both cases the name of the company was not disclosed). We then asked those same people to select, from a list of 30 common psychological traits (15 "good" and 15 "bad"), which traits they would associate with each source company.

Once the dust settled, and we had consumed enough coffee to keep the Costa Rican economy afloat, we learned:

1. BULL HAS AN AROMA—AND IT ISN'T EXACTLY CHANEL NO. 5

Not too surprisingly, the Starbucks crowd didn't like the bull sample. *Obnoxious* and *rude* were two of the four traits they assigned the bull excerpt. This makes sense, because if you are on the receiving end of bull, it's not much of a stretch to imagine that the author or speaker is pretty obnoxious and pretty rude. Less expected was the fact that the respondents associated other "bad" traits with bull, including *stubborn* and *unreliable*. And none of the 15 "good" traits were associated with the bull sample.

2. STRAIGHT TALKERS GET MORE CREDIT— PERHAPS EVEN MORE THAN THEY DESERVE

The other sample fared much better, with five of the "good" traits positively correlated with straight talk: *likable, energetic, friendly, inspiring,* and *enthusiastic*. In parallel with the bull sample, none of the 15 "bad" traits were associated with the straight talkers.

The short story is that people find straight talkers likable, and that's a big deal. In his book *The Power of Persuasion,* Robert Levine, a professor of psychology, says:

> *If you could master just one element of personal communication that is more powerful than anything . . . it is the quality of being likable. I call it the magic bullet, because if your audience likes you, they'll forgive just about everything else you do wrong. If they don't like you, you can hit every rule right on target and it doesn't matter.*

3. BIG WORDS DON'T IMPRESS

One of the reasons that business people use fifty-cent words to make a five-cent point is that they think using plain language makes them look less intelligent. That's why we say things like "Initiate project action plan" rather than "Let's get started." We fear that straightforward language might make us look dumb.

Our study showed just the opposite. *Intelligent* and *educated* were two of the 30 traits we studied. The results of the Starbucks study showed that there was no statistical difference between the straight-talk sample and the bull sample on these traits—no payoff for verbosity. This suggests that the only real admiration in bloom here is between the writer and himself.

• • •

Back to the original question: Does straight talk make a difference? Without a doubt, and in more complex ways than most of us would have thought. Your audience, the kind of people who fuel up at Starbucks every day, don't like bull. More important, when they see bull, they make negative assumptions about the person or company that spews it. When they see straight talk, they think good things about the source.

The bottom line: Bullshit eats away at your personal capital, while straight talk pays dividends.

Invest wisely.

Writing Sample 1: Corporate-Speak
*Excerpted from Gartner Group 2003 Annual Report—
source not disclosed to study participants*

Since the foundation of an agency's IT portfolio is its infrastructure, it behooves an IT-savvy council to elevate infrastructure decisions to the enterprise level. Historically, CIOs have had difficulty getting the attention of executives on this critical issue because infrastructure is usually described in terms of technology components rather than in terms of business capability. The purpose of building an enterprise IT infrastructure is to enable the sharing of information and expensive resources while creating a mechanism for cross-unit service delivery and economies of scale.

It is important to limit membership to those executives who operate at the highest level of the organization—those players with mission-critical responsibilities and budgets who head the major factions of the enterprise. The rule of thumb is to keep membership small enough to engage in meaningful dialogue and debate. All council members must have skin in the game, clout and authority to make decisions and commit resources.

Writing Sample 2: Straight Talk
*Excerpted from Amazon.com 2003 Annual Report—
source not disclosed to study participants*

In many ways, ABC Company is not a normal store. We have deep selection that is unconstrained by shelf space. We turn our inventory 19 times in a year. We personalize the store for each and every customer. We trade real estate for technology (which gets cheaper and more capable every year). We display customer reviews critical of our products. You can make a purchase with a few seconds and one click. We put used products next to new ones so you can choose. We share our prime real estate—our product detail pages—with third parties, and, if they can offer better value, we let them.

One of our most exciting peculiarities is poorly understood. People see that we're determined to offer both world-leading customer experience and the lowest possible prices. Traditional stores face a time-tested tradeoff between offering high-touch customer experience on the one hand and the lowest possible prices on the other.

2

THE SMARTEST PEOPLE
USE THE DUMBEST WORDS

If you had been a secret agent during the 1960s, one of the options you could have ordered on your car is the smoke-screen that is sent through your tailpipe to camouflage your escape. If you missed this career choice, or the 1960s, and don't care about seducing hot enemy spies of the opposite sex, you can pretend by finding any diesel Volkswagen or GM car from the 1980s and tapping the accelerator.

But business idiots have their own brand of smokescreen. If someone is onto their incompetence, there's nothing like some indigestible prose to keep everyone off their tail. And it seems that those at the highest levels of the corporate food chain (supposedly the smartest folks around) are the worst offenders. Using all those multisyllabic, supposedly smart-sounding words has exactly the opposite of the intended impact—it makes the users sound dumber than doorknobs.

Listeners know when business idiots are using the smoke-screen. And when people in your audience get lost and no longer need to focus on whatever it was you were talking about, they have time to figure out whose fault it is that they got lost.

It's yours.

WHEN IT'S OK

Jargon is the cornerstone of the Obscurity Trap. The problem *isn't* about specialized language—when used respectfully— but has a lot to do with the intent of the speaker. Every profession, even professional bowling, has some subset of words that helps its gurus share their genius in a kind of shorthand.

If you're stuck at a philatelists' convention, for example, and someone who looks as if he really ought to get a life starts talking about "Z grills" and "inverted Jennys," it's pretty much your fault for getting stuck at a stamp collectors' convention. Real experts in a real expert setting are going to sling the jargon, because it's reasonable to assume that the people in that setting are going to know what an inverted Jenny is. (No, it's not a popular new cocktail or a Kama Sutra sex position. It's one of those very rare U.S. airmail stamps from 1918 with the picture of the Curtiss Jenny airplane erroneously printed upside down.)

Courtesy of National Postal Museum/Smithsonian Institute

Real jargon—technical language among real experts—isn't the problem. Gratuitous jargon is the problem.

In many business conversations, especially when it comes to talking about esoteric stuff like strategy or the benefits of technology, real expertise is hard to pin down and worth a lot of money. So, a lot of business people fake it, and jargon is the cheapest way to do this. Audiences resent jargon, and readers give up on it. Here is a not-so-uncommon example from the website of Platform Computing:

Platform Symphony™ is leading enterprise-class software that distributes and virtualizes compute-intensive application services and processes across existing heterogeneous IT resources creating a shared, scaleable, and fault-tolerant infrastructure, delivering faster, more reliable application performance while reducing cost.

Clearly, they are targeting the impulse buyer for heterogeneous enterprise-class fault tolerant thingies.

WHEN IT'S SO BAD IT'S GOOD

Jargon is not just about using big words to make small points. Sometimes it's about using big words to make no point at all. For example, business idiots have figured out that when they don't have a real strategy, they can just string together a bunch of nonsense and make one up. And since so many other companies are in on the game, no one really notices. Which is, of course, exactly the problem.

The following is an excerpt from an internal memo sent to the employees of Coca-Cola by its former CEO, Doug Daft:

. . . Resources will be targeted at the areas of highest potential for our entire business. We will strip complexity from our operations and enhance efficiency. As we become faster, more innovative and more responsive, we will strengthen our relationship with our customers. You will, I am sure, appreciate how integration will enable us to create more growth in North America through a better go-to-market strategy that will benefit our customers, employees and system. By simplifying our business structure and focusing on (selected) channels, we will make it easier for our customers to deal with us . . .

Stunningly brilliant. What is so inspiring about this passage is that it could be used for *any* company. Coca-Cola. DuPont. Pfizer. Bubba's Bait & Tackle.

When you have nothing to say, jargon is the best way to say it.

THE WORST NEWS MAKES FOR THE BEST JARGON

When there is bad news to deliver, jargon is a business idiot's biggest ally. Business people have an incredibly difficult time delivering a tough message, and usually find a way to surround the real nuggets of information with layer upon layer of muck. In a memo announcing a global workforce reduction of 20 percent, Warner Music Group's CEO Edgar Bronfman Jr. starts off with:

We are announcing today a series of necessary restructuring steps that are critical to the future of Warner Music Group. . . . All of these steps are based on a careful and thorough analysis of all aspects of WMG's needs and operations, undertaken in close collaboration with the Com-

pany's senior management over the past few months. It is of utmost importance that we make the necessary changes as quickly as possible so that WMG can begin to move ahead with increased strength and confidence as a more competitive, agile and efficient organization."

Oh yeah, and we need to cut 20 percent of our workforce. The problem with say-nothing wind-ups is that they reduce the credibility of whatever follows. When the first few tablespoons taste like bull, don't expect the audience to think that the rest of the meal will be chateaubriand.

THE FIRST DEADLY SIN

It's pride—and jargon is an all-too-ready accomplice. Companies, and the idiots who occupy them, just can't seem to let their strengths speak for themselves. So they embellish and contour and augment things until they resemble one of those poor fools who's made one too many trips to the plastic surgeon.

We found the following in Accenture's annual report, used to describe how they are "differentiated in the marketplace":

- *We harness deep industry, process and technology expertise and unrivaled large-scale, complex change capabilities.*
- *We seamlessly integrate consulting and outsourcing capabilities across the full life cycle of business transformation*
- *We leverage our proprietary assets and global delivery network for quality, speed and lower costs*

We're not sure what mirror they're looking in, but do they actually think this makes them look good? Get rid of all cosmetic language, and give the truth a chance to come out and be seen.

THE BULL SPOTTER'S GUIDE

The Bullfighter software we mentioned earlier included a dictionary of 350 words that qualified as jargon. Obviously, it was a highly dangerous and scientific task to compile this many bull words. Please recognize that this effort was conducted by trained professionals with deep experience in administering and recognizing bull and that we would recommend prudence and moderation to anyone who seeks to follow in our footsteps. We would also recommend a pair of those knee-high rubber boots.

At any rate, to populate the dictionary for the Bullfighter software, we conducted a survey among more than 10,000 consultants under the guise of the Serious Bull Contest. The prize—a weekend at the California Academy of Tauromaquia (that's a real bullfighting school, of the nonlethal sort)—drew 9,672 entries from several hundred of the most rabid jargon haters in the world. For a partial list of terms that made it into Bullfighter, see the Resources section at the end of this book. Words that earned "most reviled" status appear on the following page.

Once you've used a tool like Bullfighter or seen a list like this, you'll start policing your own language for useless jargon. In fact, the long-term impact of the software was meant to be a kind of behavioral modification. The always-visible red-and-black bull's-head button on our word processing toolbar was as much a deterrent as anyone needed to lose a lot of the bull.

STOAS (SOME THOUGHTS ON ACRONYMS)

Another insidious form of jargon is the acronym. Some acronyms are useful and welcome. Nobody wants to go *self-contained underwater breathing apparatus* diving, but SCUBA

Serious Bull Contest: The Best of the Worst

Best of breed — The whole breeding thing seems to come from a testosterone-driven compulsion to prove that a product has survived some sort of Darwinian natural selection process. Usually you'll hear this from out-of-shape IT guys who spend a lot of evenings eating french fries at their desk and don't do much in the way of breeding.

Center of excellence — Vortex of incomparable splendor, hub of magnificence, apex of awesomeness, whatever. No one likes anyone who works in any of these.

Frictionless — The consulting version of anti-aging cream or the exercise-free fitness program. You should run quickly in the opposite direction when the topic turns to a "frictionless" transition plan, for example.

Out of pocket — "Unavailable," but implies a kind of mysterious inaccessibility that leaves open the possibility that you'll be on safari or doing another one of those Mt. Everest jaunts.

Paradigm shift — Business idiots use this to refer to anything done differently. Darwin's theory of evolution and Copernicus's discovery that the earth revolves around the sun caused paradigm shifts. Outsourcing your company's payroll may be a good idea, but if it was sold as a "paradigm shift" you paid too much.

Results-driven — The opposite of this is "for the sheer hell of it," but because so few business proposals have succeeded by describing that a project will be done "for the sheer hell of it," this is a good expression to lose.

Socialize — Not in the familiar sense of "to socialize with friends," but as a kinder and gentler and seriously misleading substitute for "propagandize."

diving is popular. And even if you don't know what "SCUBA" stands for, because most people don't, everyone knows what it means. But what the world needs now is another SCUBA—a **S**ystem to **C**lean **U**p **B**ogus **A**cronyms.

Acronyms for the sake of acronyms breed acrimony and mass confusion. The Internet Acronyms Dictionary (www .gaarde.org) lists hundreds of examples, including "K," short for the long and ponderous "OK," which replaced the toner-wasting and interminable "okay." Others include "APPLE" (Arrogance Produces Profit-Losing Entity) and "ARE" (Acronym-Rich Environment). The problem with these is not when we use them inside our companies, but when we start thinking they are real words that mean something to people on the outside.

What does "PSR" mean to you? To musicians, it's one model of Yamaha's electronic keyboard. Activist doctors would say "Physicians for Social Responsibility." Here are results from the first 60 pages of an Internet search for "PSR":

> Physicians for Social Responsibility
> Pacific School of Religion
> Price/Sales Ratio
> Periodontal Screening & Recording
> Political Science Resources
> Papers on Social Representations
> Packet Status Register
> Partido Socialista Revolucionario
> Password Storage & Retrieval
> PlayStation Reporter
> Product Specific Requirements
> Primary Science Review
> Professional Sportscar Racing
> Paris Short-Term Rentals

Program Status Register
Portuguese Study Review
Princely States Report
Personal Service Request
Problem-Solution-Results
Platform Support Rods
Protective Services Result
Passenger Service Representative
Product Specific Release
Philosophy Student Resources
Pray for Specific Results
Panther Software & Research
Program Security Representative
Psychosocial Rehabilitation Services
Paternal Sex Ration
Post-Secondary Recruitment
Public Services Redefinition
Peters Seed & Research
Powersoft Report
Phi Sigma Rho
Patron Saint Records
Pacific Southwest Region
Patient Services Representative
Pacific-Sierra Research
People's Soviet Republic
PowerStroke Registry
Polarimetric Scanning Radiometer
PBP5 (Penicillin-building protein 5) Synthesis Repressor

For PSR (people still reading), brand building and clarity are two PSRs (pretty smart reasons) not to use an obscure acronym.

KICK THE HABIT

Jargon is the foundation of obscurity. It's only part of the long slide into idiocy, but if you want to connect with your audience and persuade them, word choice is a good place to start.

To help you kick the jargon habit, we don't have a long list of writing tips, style guides, reference manuals, or even hypnotist referrals to offer. We tried all that and it didn't work. But we did learn a thing or two that might help. On our straight-talk crusade, we came to realize that awareness breeds contempt. Once we started thinking about jargon, we started to see it everywhere. And we started to hate what we saw—including the garbage that spewed from our own mouths and keyboards.

So the single most important thing you can do to kick the jargon habit is to develop a deep and vitriolic hatred of it. If you don't do too well with anger management, then a strong dislike will be OK. Once you become aware of how disrespectful it is to your audience, you will start to notice it more often.

Then the hard part starts. We don't use jargon because we are moronic jerks trying to piss off the people we most need to impress (well, *usually* not). We use jargon because it's a shortcut. Because sometimes it's just easier to lapse into vagary and verbosity than to work our way through to clarity and crispness.

Fight this urge. And if you get withdrawal symptoms, like the fear that comes when you make a point that is starkly clear and revealing, it's good to have your own support group. Other jargonaholics who are suffering through the same thing.

Kick the jargon habit, and the obscurity trap gets a lot less menacing.

3

SIZE MATTERS, BUT NOT HOW YOU THINK

I will be brief. Not nearly so brief as Salvador Dali, who gave the world's shortest speech. He said "I will be so brief I have already finished," and he sat down.

—EDWARD O. WILSON

Back when you were in grade school, your teachers probably gave reading assignments. Sometimes they were long, sometimes they were short, but no one complained about the short ones.

Then on the weekend you went to church, synagogue, or some other place where guilt was administered to you by a professional guilt-administrator while you were dressed up and miserable in your state of extreme cuteness. You heard a sermon. It might have been 55 minutes about why you should do unto others as you would have them do unto you, or maybe it was 10 minutes on the same topic. Why someone needed to do 55 minutes of this stuff unto you is something you could never figure out, but the 10-minute one got rave reviews. Short and sweet. Everyone got the message.

Length has its advantages, but when it comes to words, sentences, documents, and presentations, shortness is your ally.

A GLORIOUSLY SHORT HISTORY OF SHORTNESS

The Battle of Gettysburg was a bloody victory for the Union and marked the beginning of the end of the Confederacy. More than 45,000 soldiers died. (The U.S. population in 1863 was under 35 million. Imagine a battle where 325,000 U.S. soldiers died today and you start to get the idea.) By any measure, this was a critical time for the country and a time for well-chosen words from the president.

Lincoln, however, wasn't the main speaker at the dedication of the cemetery—noted orator Edward Everett was. Few people thought the president was much of a speaker. Lincoln's address was astoundingly short, 270 words that described perfectly the sentiment of the president and the nation.

Please don't skip this part. It's worth reading. Remember, it's short.

Four score and seven years ago our fathers brought forth on this continent a new nation, conceived in liberty and dedicated to the proposition that all men are created equal.

Now we are engaged in a great civil war, testing whether that nation, or any nation so conceived and so dedicated, can long endure. We are met on a great battlefield of that war. We have come to dedicate a portion of that field, as a final resting place for those who here gave their lives that that nation might live. It is altogether fitting and proper that we should do this.

But, in a larger sense, we cannot dedicate, we cannot consecrate, we cannot hallow this ground. The brave men, living and dead, who struggled here have consecrated it far above our poor power to add or detract. The world will little note nor long remember what we say here, but it can never forget what they did here. It is for us the living, rather, to be dedicated here to the unfinished work which they who fought here have thus far so nobly advanced. It is rather for us to be here dedicated to the great task remaining before us—that from these honored dead we take increased devotion to that cause for which they gave the last full measure of devotion; that we here highly resolve that these dead shall not have died in vain; that this nation, under God, shall have a new birth of freedom; and that government of the people, by the people, for the people, shall not perish from the earth.

November 19, 1863; Gettysburg, Pennsylvania

Despite Lincoln's humility, the world noted what was said, and it continues to be remembered as possibly one of the greatest speeches ever made. Most people don't remember that it was so brief, because Lincoln said everything that needed to be said, and with great eloquence. Then he stopped talking.

At the same ceremony Edward Everett delivered a 13,500-word address that took about two hours. We would have reprinted it here, but we figured that you probably remembered it.

DOCUMENT OBESITY

There's a reason we get beat up with hour-long presentations and four-minute voicemails with endings that no one ever lis-

(Source: Library of Congress)

Edward Everett

tens to. Length implies that some work went into the production. It takes time to write 50 pages about something, but if we turn in five pages, it looks as though we haven't put much time into the job.

High school teachers use this technique: A term paper must be 20 pages and have two pages of footnotes, from at least five different sources. In some ways, this is a useful guideline for high school students who might have no way of knowing how many pages it would take to cover topic X. It also weeds out the students who don't want to do any real work, because it's (slightly) easier to crank out five pages of garbage than 15 pages.

But guidelines like these are not so useful in the business world where the objective isn't to spend a minimum of 12 hours in the library. The objective is to connect, convince, and make money.

A lot of high school students go on to grow up, get jobs, and make presentations. We probably forget 90 percent of what we learn in high school, but stupid length requirements for documents are one of those things that stick with us forever. That's not a good thing.

COPY, PASTE, BLOAT

Length is supposed to imply insight, but usually the opposite is true. If you talk to a great editor, she'll tell you that it's much more difficult to write a great short article than a long one. Business idiots don't really edit. That 100-slide PowerPoint travesty inherited its bloat from the six other bloated presentations that were pasted together at the last minute. If someone had put real work into it, most of those slides would have been removed.

One culprit? Our friends Copy and Paste. In the age of the typewriter, you had to read—and hear in your mind—whatever it was you were putting on the page. A long paper really *was* an achievement. No longer. Software makes it easy to recycle paragraphs, documents, and presentations. There ought to be separate commands for "Copy Thoughtful Material" and "Copy Bloated Crap," but unfortunately there's one command that brings it all together. Business is obsessed with not "reinventing the wheel" and discourages anyone from wasting much time crafting anything from scratch. (So much for creativity.) More than anything, software has made it no more difficult to create long documents than shorter ones.

WE SHALL FIGHT . . .

Beyond shortness in length, the best speakers also seem to get away with a lot shorter words (those of the one- and two-syllable variety).

Winston Churchill was a master of English. He could turn a phrase in a way that made the world sit up and take notice— at a time when it really needed to start paying attention. There's a momentum, in some of Churchill's best known passages, in which the listener finds one resonant thought after another. We are pulled forward irresistibly by his unambiguous language and taut prose:

> *We shall not flag or fail. We shall go on to the end. We shall fight in France, we shall fight on the seas and oceans, we shall fight with growing confidence and growing strength in the air, we shall defend our island, whatever the cost may be, we shall fight on the beaches, we shall fight on the landing grounds, we shall fight in the fields and in the streets, we shall fight in the hills; we shall never surrender.*
>
> Speech to the House of Commons; June 4, 1940

This is among the most quoted speeches in the history of the twentieth century, and deservedly so, because even today, his words raise the hair on the listener's neck. There's not a four-syllable word anywhere and nothing left to ponder. His words impressed the world, rattled Hitler, and convinced Franklin Delano Roosevelt to create the Lend-Lease program.

None of us may confront a threat of that magnitude. If we do, though, it's good to know that we can always dust off those one-syllable words and send them into action—even at work.

THE DOCTOR IS IN

In 1946, Dr. Rudolf Flesch devised his Flesch Reading Ease Scale. Through research, he created a method to calculate the difficulty of reading a section of text, as measured by the education level required of the reader. What he found was that long sentences and long words demanded more education and effort of the reader. Sentences longer than 21 words proved challenging. When the average syllable count of the words approached two, reading ease declined.

This sounds harsh, but remember that most English words are one syllable.

He created a complex formula to tally what he called a document's Readability Score. The scores are plotted on a scale from 0 to 100, with 100 being the easiest to read. Here are some examples Flesch calculated to show his formula in practice:

Comics	92
Sports Illustrated	63
Wall Street Journal	43
IRS tax code	−6

Different scores are appropriate for different audiences. And it's next to impossible to write something that scores a 100 (outside of See Spot run), so we wouldn't recommend shooting for this kind of simplicity. But in general, your writing should score above 35 if you want the average business audience to understand and actually finish reading it.

The real issue with long-windedness is that it prevents you from connecting with your audience. Just as endless sentences filled with jargon frustrate us and cause us to worry about missing the point, a crisp and short phrase makes us feel on top of things. We get it.

This is different from the last two-hour corporate presentation you attended where the idiot speaking had to remind everyone of the outline every half hour or so. Short articles and presentations don't put such a burden on the audience to figure out how they are organized. Most people won't make the effort to figure it all out anyway.

THE LONG AND SHORT OF IT ALL

Here's the real skinny on size:

- Short presentations pack a punch. (Guys like Lincoln used this technique.)
- Short sentences are more memorable than long ones. (Mix and match, but 21 words starts to become long for most people.)
- One-syllable words build momentum and give the long ones impact. (Churchill knew a lot of long words, but when it mattered most he shelved those in favor of the short ones.)

The great enemy of clear language is insincerity. When there is a gap between one's real and one's declared aims, one turns as it were instinctively to long words and exhausted idioms, like a cuttlefish squirting out ink.

—GEORGE ORWELL, *ANIMAL FARM*

4

IT DEPENDS ON WHAT
THE MEANING OF "IS" IS

We agree with George. There is entirely too much indiscriminate squirting going on out there. Take Bill Clinton's Grand Jury testimony, for example:

ATTORNEY: Whether or not Mr. Bennett knew of your relationship with Ms. Lewinsky, the statement that there was "no sex of any kind in any manner, shape or form, with President Clinton," was an utterly false statement. Is that correct?

CLINTON: It depends upon what the meaning of the word "is" is. If the—if he—if "is" means "is and never has been and is not"—that is one thing. If it means there is none, that was a completely true statement.

When it comes to evasiveness, President Bill Clinton's answer at the grand jury investigation wasn't pretty. But most business communications aren't far behind.

Business idiots have become commitophobes. They live in constant fear of being held accountable for something tangible and throw together generic statements that sound vaguely positive but really say nothing: "Our software has enabled customers to achieve quantifiable return on their investment within a brief timeframe." Yes, this is from a real-life press release. We assume it was a positive ROI, but who knows. What timeframe? We don't know.

Not all masters of evasiveness work in the private sector. In an editorial, "The Food Pyramid Scheme," *The New York Times* found obscurity alive and well in the federal government's revision of dietary guidelines for Americans. A recent report had confirmed that sugary foods crowded out nutritious ones and encouraged obesity. Pretty straightforward. But look what the newspaper has to say about how the government panel described its findings:

> *When the 13 doctors and professors on the panel distilled the evidence into nine tips for healthy eating, they didn't mention sugar. Instead, they proposed a guideline that reads, unhelpfully, "Choose carbohydrates wisely for good health."*
>
> *To achieve this level of obscurity, the committee in effect had to break with five sets of guidelines, dating to 1980, that addressed the sugar issue with direct injunctions like "Avoid too much sugar." . . .*

With obesity an epidemic, the public desperately needs authoritative advice. The government could restore some of the credibility it lost when it selected panel members with ties to industry, and fulfill its mission to promote health—not the sugar lobby—by rewriting the advice on sugar. How about this: "Reduce added sugars."

The New York Times, editorial, Sept. 1, 2004

In business, the real epidemic is obscurity. Only the best leaders seem to be able to resist turning into a mound of Jell-O when it comes time to actually say something that could be taken as a stand. One of the most celebrated? Jack Welch: "We will be number one or two in every business we're in, or we will fix it, close it or sell it." Any questions? Imagine if Welch had spent more time hanging out with business idiots. He could have come up with something like "We will be ranked among the top companies in our industry, unless there are unforeseen changes in the competitive landscape that affect our competitive capabilities related to strategic investments, acquisitions, or strategic execution. In that case maybe we'll be some other number."

Welch is the rare role model—evasiveness wasn't in his vocabulary.

EVASIVENESS CAN BE BAD NEWS

Sometimes people are evasive because they haven't thought things through. Although this makes for bad writing, we all do it sometimes. But sometimes people are evasive because they really have something to hide.

We took a look at the letters to the shareholders in the annual reports of two types of companies: well-respected and admired companies, and companies recently investigated for financial scandals. We calculated the Flesch Reading Ease scores (the higher the score, the clearer the writing) shown in the tables.

This doesn't mean that everyone with a low Flesch score should be prosecuted, but it does suggest that evasiveness, the third component of the Obscurity Trap, is worth looking into. If we can't understand something, that may be because someone doesn't want us to understand.

All of this puts the Obscurity Trap is an even harsher light. We saw in the Starbucks study that readers formed negative views of companies—and people—who wrote in an obscure corporate voice. Our survey of some of the "least admired" companies suggests that those participants in our study at that Atlanta Starbucks were onto something. If it sounds like bullshit, it just might be.

Perhaps this shouldn't be so surprising. If you have something to hide, it's not so shocking that evasive language would creep into your communications. For example, Ken Lay and Jeff Skilling's final letter to Enron shareholders (Enron Annual Report, 2000) often defies comprehension. An excerpt:

> *We have robust networks of strategic assets that we own or have contractual access to, which give us greater flexibility and speed to reliably deliver widespread logistical solutions. . . . We have metamorphosed from an asset-based pipeline and power generating company to a marketing and logistics company whose biggest assets are its well-established business approach and its innovative people.*

Enron had an indecipherable letter to shareholders because its business *was* indecipherable. The officers had something to hide, and evasive language played into that.

STRAIGHT TALK OR SCANDAL?

CEOs OF ADMIRED COMPANIES
Letters to Shareholders

CEO (*COMPANY, FISCAL YEAR*)	FLESCH READING EASE SCORE
Lou Gerstner (*IBM, 2001*)	45
Jack Welch (*General Electric, 2000*)	44
Larry Page/Sergey Brin (*Google, 2004*)	44
Meg Whitman (*eBay, 2003*)	44
Warren Buffett (*Berkshire Hathaway, 2003*)	43
Jeff Bezos (*Amazon.com, 2003*)	40

CEOs OF COMPANIES ASSOCIATED WITH SCANDALS
Letters to Shareholders

CEO (*COMPANY, FISCAL YEAR*)	FLESCH READING EASE SCORE
Dennis Kozlowski (*Tyco, 2001*)	29
Sam Waksal (*ImClone, 2001*)	22
Richard Scrushy (*HealthSouth, 2001*)	20
Ken Lay/Jeffrey Skilling (*Enron, 2000*)	18
John J. Rigas (*Adelphia, 2000*)	18
Gary Winnick (*Global Crossing, 2001*)	17
Richard Grasso (*NYSE, 2002*)	17

OK, enough with the negative. Here's an excerpt from one of the least evasive letters to shareholders we've seen, the 2004 letter from Google:

Google is not a conventional company. We do not intend to become one. Throughout Google's evolution as a privately held company, we have managed Google differently. We have also emphasized an atmosphere of creativity and challenge, which has helped us provide unbiased, accurate and free access to information for those who rely on us around the world.

Many companies have suffered from unreasonable speculation, small initial share float, and boom-bust cycles that hurt them and their investors in the long run. We believe that an auction-based IPO will minimize these problems.

Although we may discuss long-term trends in our business, we do not plan to give earnings guidance in the traditional sense. We are not able to predict our business within a narrow range for each quarter.

A management team distracted by a series of short-term targets is as pointless as a dieter stepping on a scale every half hour.

We provide many unusual benefits for our employees, including meals free of charge, doctors and washing machines. We are careful to consider the long-term advantages to the company of these benefits. Expect us to add benefits rather than pare them down over time. We believe it is easy to be penny wise and pound foolish with respect to benefits that can save employees considerable time and improve their health and productivity.

Don't be evil. We believe strongly that in the long term,

we will be better served—as shareholders and in all other ways—by a company that does good things for the world even if we forgo some short-term gains. This is an important aspect of our culture and is broadly shared within the company.

II

The Anonymity Trap

You're only given a little spark of madness. You mustn't lose it.
—ROBIN WILLIAMS

Is This Your Eulogy?

We're here today to celebrate the life of my direct report, Ned.

*I had the good fortune of managing Ned for the last 20 years.
And I can tell you, without hesitation, that Ned was a class-
act corporate citizen.*

*Those of you who manage people, you know what I mean.
You really appreciate the ones who play by the rules.
The ones who aren't always trying to do something to
stand out.
Who just do their job, day in and day out, quietly and
peacefully.
And that was Ned.*

*He always fit in—never made any trouble.
In fact, most of the time, we never even knew he was around.
Just the kind of employee every company loves to have—the
go-along-to-get-along type.*

*Scripture says, "The meek shall inherit the earth."
And I'd like to think this is his chance to shine.*

*Rest in peace, uhhh . . . Ned.
Yes, Ned.
Rest in peace.*

DON'T BE NED

Nobody in corporate America wants this eulogy. But this is where things are headed. One of the major reasons that business people speak like idiots is that they have lost their human voice. We have allowed our personalities to be systematically neutered and spayed into oblivion.

We have business schools that churn out clones; an epidemic of political correctness that demands every sneeze be approved by a 12-person committee; corporate scandals that have eliminated even the slightest appetite for risk; and company standards for everything from presentations and e-mail signatures to clothing and performance ratings.

It's no wonder most of us feel that a personality isn't the kind of thing you'd want to bring to work. Yet by eliminating personality, we've undermined our ability to connect with an audience. Once you check your uniqueness at the door, there's no reason anyone should remember you. Or listen to you. And there's no reason your eulogy won't look like the pathetic thing that opened this chapter.

This is the Anonymity Trap. While on the outside every organization is trying to "differentiate" itself through advertising and marketing, on the inside, it's pushing everyone to be the same. Businesses love clones because they can all be trained the same way, be paid the same way, and eventually behave the same way. If a clone leaves, a business can always hire another at the same salary. Managers love clones because there's a kind of economy of scale in managing people who produce what the manager expects. Just as it's easier for *manufacturing* systems to pump out standardized products, it's also easier for *management* systems to pump out standardized people. The moment we arrive at our first job, the pressure's on: these are the rules; now, conform.

And we go along with it. Ever listen to yourself on a business call, and notice how different you sound from when you're on a personal call? We put on that special, sophisticated business voice as soon as we get to work because everybody else does it, too, and subconsciously, we're afraid not to. People might not take us seriously.

Fortunately, the great tide of conformity has created more than clones—it has created an opportunity for you to put your personality onstage. All that sameness makes it even more special when someone finds a way to stand out. All you have to do is expose the human being beneath the corporate shrink-wrap.

WINNING THE ANONYMITY GAME

If you want to win the anonymity game, there are four techniques that can make or break your chances:

- **Templates.** Sure, they're convenient, but the worst deal you can make is to trade your awesome personality for a bunch of recycled presentation slides. This goes beyond software; it includes the general fill-in-the-blank mentality that idiots have about everything in business. Idiots fall over themselves "leveraging" everyone else's materials and filling in the blanks in prefabricated presentations. If you want your audience to sit up and take notice, you have to stamp your work with your own uniqueness and personality.
- **Polish.** No, not the people in that large, cold country in Eastern Europe. They can't help you. We're referring to the kind of polish business idiots apply to presentations and messages that makes them sound like stuffy memos

instead of something anyone would bother to listen to. Perfection and predictability will get you good grades in that business school presentation class, but to your audience they scream "prefabricated," "rehearsed," and "canned." Lose some of that polish and show a bit of that human imperfection.

- **Humor.** People love humor, and they go out of their way to listen to other people who have a great sense of humor. Unfortunately for all of us, most people who have a sense of humor leave it in the parking lot when they go to work. But you don't have to. And you don't have to be a stand-up comic to use humor, in a smart and professional way, to beat the Anonymity Trap.

- **Picking up the damn phone.** Business idiots cling to anonymity. Better to be one of 500 e-mails in someone's inbox than to actually engage in a conversation. If you want to spend a career flying below the radar, dull e-mails and conference calls with 20 faceless people are the fastest path to that gold watch. But if you want to beat the Anonymity Trap, you need to reject the invisibility that comes with these invisible media.

You may be wondering, "Why on earth would I take that risk? There's no reward, and I can just keep a low profile the way I do now."

But there *are* a couple of great rewards. You'll increase your ability to do the one thing that is fundamental to your career: persuade others. If you've ever been laid off, "re-org'd" out of a high post, or shuffled from one department to another, you know how fleeting the artificial power that comes with a title can be. The only power you have comes from your ability to persuade others to do what you want—in essence, your personality.

Equally important is the liberation you'll feel once you shed the straitjacket you've been wearing. Work doesn't seem like work so much when you can be who you really are.

And then you can stop worrying about that eulogy thing.

5

YOU'VE BEEN
TEMPLATIZED

For the guy who's mass-producing beer bottles, uniformity is a good thing. It's great when all of the labels are on right-side up and the caps stay on during shipment. The ultimate accomplishment for the guy making beer bottles—no, they're not individually hand-blown—is to keep it boring and predictable. For the last century, business has been focused on making things boring and predictable, which is high praise in the world of statistics and quality control. But then we started automating everything around us, and soon came the next big thing in mass production: business communications. And *boring* and *predictable* present a bit of a problem here.

Let's start with presentations. There's a lot of time to be saved by standardizing presentations. No one has to think about the basic elements of layout, because the presentation wizard does that. No one has to think about how to organize a presentation, because the auto-content outline generator does that. There's no reason to sweat the different pieces of the presentation, because they're all right there in a drop-down list box. Got a question? The online "paper-clip guy" can point you to a standardized answer. In a rush? Our pals Copy and Paste can help. With friends like these, who needs to create anything?

This makes life easier for us as presenters, but it also makes it easier for us as listeners—to tune out. The brain doesn't pay much attention to all of this homogenized information. A set of 20 uniform text slides doesn't interest us. We like variety. There's meaning in things that are different.

Templates that let us quickly churn out presentations steal our chance to be creative. They force brilliant and stupid ideas into the same format—and scream conformity.

CAN POWERPOINT KILL?

The biggest risk of these dull, templatized presentations can be more than boredom. On February 1, 2003, the space shuttle *Columbia* disintegrated on re-entry into the earth's atmosphere, killing all seven astronauts on board. NASA's Columbia Accident Investigation Board concluded that the cause was damage from foam debris from the external launch tank, which struck the shuttle's left wing 81.9 seconds after launch.

Did NASA know this was a possibility before it happened? Unfortunately, they should have.

On January 24, 2003, the week before the disaster, a Debris Assessment Team delivered a formal briefing on their findings, using—what else?—a PowerPoint presentation. The team warned of the risks, but for some reason, the message never got through. After the fact, NASA admitted that Power-Point might have played a key role in the communications failure. One of the team's slides is shown here; there's little

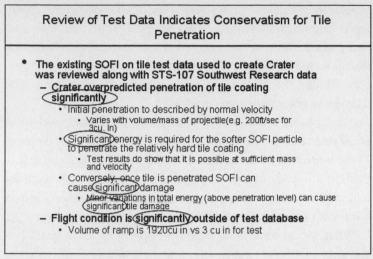

Slide: NASA

wonder the Debris Assessment Team wasn't able to move NASA to action.

The most scathing critic of this presentation is information design guru Edward Tufte, who has said the structure of this key slide makes it difficult to get the real message.* NASA knew that the actual impact of the debris during the *Columbia* launch was far greater than anything modeled in an earlier analysis (called "Crater" and mentioned on the slide). The analysis also showed that Spray-On Foam Insulation ("SOFI") could cause "significant" damage if it were to penetrate the hard tile on the space shuttle exterior. Unfortunately, for anyone trying to figure out how serious the situation was, the lethal truth was buried in the lowest level bullet points. The fact that the Crater analysis really didn't apply to *Columbia's* damage appears in the second to last line: "Flight condition is

* Edward Tufte, *The Cognitive Style of PowerPoint,* Graphics Press, Cheshire, CT, 2003.

significantly outside of test database." Moreover, the sterile word "significant" appears five times. It's not an alarming word, but in this case we know that there was a real reason for alarm. In the last line, "significantly" actually meant 400 percent. Maybe the slide should have had only one line: "The damage is potentially catastrophic."

The Columbia Accident Investigation Board stopped short of saying that PowerPoint caused the *Columbia* disaster. There were other issues, mostly organizational. But the investigation group did devote a page of its report to Tufte's explanation. The compressed, formulaic writing that goes hand in hand with PowerPoint slides obscured a critical message.

What would have been a better approach? NASA had photographs of similar (but much lesser) impact damage on other space shuttles. High-resolution photos of the actual damage would have made the point dramatically.

SURRENDER TO THE SOFTWARE

There's no rule that presentations have to look like this, and it's a stretch to blame PowerPoint for a dull or, in this case, dangerously misleading presentation. Someone used the software badly. But business idiots are the sheep that use any shortcut available to automate their voice, and PowerPoint is a prime example. Templates steal your opportunity for individual expression. It's one way of surrendering your creative powers to software, and a sure way to fall into the Anonymity Trap.

Start your presentation with a story. Start it with a dramatic prop. Start with an interview. Start with a video or movie clip. Start with a photo of a sport utility vehicle flipped on its roof after an accident. Something. Anything!

Or start with a slide that has some version of "Insert Title

Here" in the middle. Just don't expect your audience to remember you or your message. You've been templatized.

TEMPLATE HATERS' GUIDE

To avoid the Anonymity Trap, learn to recognize templates. Then lace up your track shoes and run the other way. Power-Point is an obvious arch-villain, because it can create your presentation outline and even select a color scheme. Fill in a few specifics and presto—dull presentation that conforms to dull standards. But dull templates aren't limited to Power-Point.

CORPORATE MEMO
It's good to have the company name somewhere, but the customary fluffy opening about how great the company is and how the execs owe it all to the worker bees sounds contrived. How about starting with a controversial statement? Or just something unexpected? We would all read a memo that begins "Are you about to trash this memo? If so, good!"

VOICEMAIL
Dump the implied template. "This is a voice message from Dave going to all of the fine managers who make our firm great. I'm sending this voice message to alert you to an e-mail . . ." Everyone knows it's a voice message, and everyone knows they have received it. Get creative. Deliver it as a radio broadcast, interview, or commercial. If you're not feeling that edgy, try starting with the main point and ending very shortly afterward, like a breaking news story. Send it yourself to avoid the inane string of "forwarding" preambles that happens when your secretary's assistant's assistant ends up sending all of your voicemails. This is the *throne effect*—the

message has trickled down from so far up the corporate food chain that it had to come through x layers to actually reach workers down there in the primordial ooze.

E-MAIL

Make your subject line memorable. Pretend you're writing a news lead and you have to get people to read it and pay for it. Get the main points in your message near the top—never bury them in an attachment. No one opens attachments. Virus scanners sometimes delete these anyway. Before you click Send, refer to Chapter 8, "Pick Up the Damn Phone." Should you even be sending e-mail, anyway?

NEWSLETTER

Brand it. Give your newsletter a name, an editorial style, and a logo—logos are easy and inexpensive. Don't talk about the newsletter in the newsletter. Start with a note from some guy who's been with the company a year, not the CEO. Start it with a letter from a customer. Publish real letters from co-workers and colleagues.

PRESENTATIONS

Apart from the obvious technical stuff—don't let the software create your presentation—there are many little things you can do to avoid the implicit templates that are part of corporate life. Title your presentation as though it were a best-selling thriller. Avoid bulleted lists and SGPs (Stupid Generic Photographs—see page 62). Get out from behind the podium. Finish ahead of schedule. Tell a story that's not in your slides. Use only photos in your slides. Move technical data to a technical data document. Never show an organization chart unless your presentation is about the new organization chart. If someone's introducing you, give him or her license to have fun. Introduce yourself with a smile-inducing story—not a long, pretentious title.

More generally, don't reuse someone else's presentation. If you copy and paste from the work of someone who has been infected by the template disease, you risk getting infected yourself. A blank sheet of paper may seem pretty intimidating in the Age of Copy and Paste, but guys like Lincoln and Churchill struggled by using just that.

WE'RE OFF TO LOSE THE WIZARD

The good news is that you can almost always do an end run around the evil forces of templatization and come up with something better. Most people won't, which will make whatever you're doing even more interesting.

You don't have to skydive into the conference room to make an impact. All you have to do is avoid the usual traps. Business idiots are template addicts. Write original stuff, get original photos and artwork—buy access to a royalty-free website or put your graphics team to work—and break a couple of rules (it almost doesn't matter which ones). Look outside of your PC or office for new templates. Improvisation? Documentary? Guest speaker? The mind is always looking for new stuff. Make sure your audience is always finding it.

Special Bonus Feature: SGPs

The cornerstone of any idiot's presentation or newsletter is the Stupid Generic Photograph (SGP). These add mass without content, and often at no additional cost.

Experts point out that selecting just the right SGP is a carefully honed skill. It takes a keen eye to recognize an image that can be used absolutely anywhere. You want to use an inoffensive image—one that displays a distinct absence of emotion. No one should be able to get any meaning out of these pictures, or you've screwed up.

The ultimate goal is for the subjects in the photos to appear deeply concerned and very intellectual and busy. It's important to convey self-importance, so it won't work to show a bunch of young guys smiling at each other at Starbucks. It's got to be serious business.

Distinction is obviously a challenge with the high standards around the effort to be so standard. While some of the more avant-garde SGP artists have experimented with subjects in real settings, the acknowledged masters avoid this. You will recognize some of the classics of this genre: waving

or pointing a Montblanc pen, the handshake outside the taxi, the swinging briefcase, the flippy-type cell phone in the subway station. And never forget the concerned, thoughtful gaze.

While a complete guide to the techniques employed by SGP artists would fill many pages, here are a few key elements of any good SGP strategy:

- **Ethnic balance.** The all-time classic SGP is the black/white handshake—this can't be used often enough. In group pictures, consider using unexpected ethnic touches for effect. For example, if it's an NBA huddle, SGP experts recommend inserting a pale white guy wearing a yarmulke.

- **Gender balance.** Always 50-50. Always. If it's a baby shower, find a guy to lean in and look completely absorbed. In the business meeting, a woman should always be giving the presentation. But be sure she's wearing an impeccably tailored suit that her glass-ceiling salary wouldn't possibly allow.

- **Eyeglasses.** Most SGP experts recommend eyeglasses for people over 40. Especially those fashionable little Italian jobbies you only find in the advertising industry.

- **Pointing.** In real life, presentations are dull and user manuals are irrelevant. In an SGP, all written materials are fascinating. Everything written is too important not to call a meeting about. If you study the SGPs produced by the real masters, you'll see a lot of pointing going on.

- **Angles.** Make sure people are leaning, reclining, or doing something other than sitting there rod straight. If you've completely blown it and everyone is just sitting there looking fake and boring, you can always tilt the whole picture to create the illusion that it's exciting. Sometimes you just need to tilt it and hope for the best. Remember, office work is boring, and we're going for excitement here. Serious excitement, though.

• **Contemporary SGP trends.** Conventional SGP taboos are being challenged today. Previously, male pattern baldness was unimaginable in an SGP. Today, however, innovators are pushing the frontiers of scalp exposure. In one of the most daring experiments yet, certain SGP artists have begun to show bald people having fun at work. Laughter, joy, and all sorts of similar carryings-on. Imagine that.

THE POWER OF
IMPERFECTION

Courtesy of Hulton Archive/
CBS Photo Archive/Getty Images

November 22, 1963.

At 2:37 P.M. CBS news editor Ed Bliss, Jr., hands anchorman Walter Cronkite an AP wire report. Cronkite takes a long second to read it to himself before intoning: "From Dallas, Texas, the flash, apparently official. President Kennedy died at 1:00 P.M. Central Standard Time, two o'clock Eastern Standard Time." He pauses and looks at the studio clock. "Some thirty-eight minutes ago." Momentarily losing his composure, Cronkite winces, removes his eyeglasses, and clears his throat before resuming with the observation that

Vice President Lyndon Johnson will presumably take the oath of office to become the thirty-sixth president of the United States.

—THE MUSEUM OF BROADCAST COMMUNICATIONS

KENNEDY AND CRONKITE

What has been called the "most moving and historic" passage in broadcast history—and it's hard to say otherwise—was a sharp departure from the rehearsed and stiff television of its era. News of the shooting broke an hour earlier, and there were unconfirmed reports that President Kennedy had been fatally wounded. Cronkite himself had delivered that momentous news, breaking into the soap opera *As the World Turns*. But it was this segment that got inside of everyone watching. Decades later, it has the same effect. There's no doubt that Kennedy's death would have moved the nation no matter who reported it, and others did, nonstop for days, but Cronkite's broadcast is the one of record. Why?

There's a brief but riveting pause while Cronkite reads the wire report. *What's he reading?* It might have been that glance back at the studio clock, or the uncharacteristic clearing of his throat—news anchors have always been hired for their seamless, unflappable delivery. *Why did he have to look at the clock?* Maybe it was the removal of the eyeglasses. *No one ever does that on TV.*

Whatever it was, the whole nation saw that the most even-keeled guy in the United States, in a decade when men were never caught weeping in public, was on the verge of tears on national television. Walter Cronkite! Choked up on the most important broadcast of his career. It gave the whole audience license to share their grief. Cronkite went on to become a legend in broadcast news.

FROM ARTIFICIAL TO AUTHENTIC

Avoiding the Anonymity Trap is all about making a personal connection with your audience. Templates are your enemy. Humor is your ally. At some basic level, though, the audience is going to decide whether you actually care about the topic or are simply standing there to read from a script.

The polish we apply to all our performances is one of the downfalls of business presentations. Whatever efficiencies come from cue cards, notes, or scripts, they make it obvious that what we're saying is coming from the page rather than from our hearts. The listener knows that this presentation is a one-sided experience—it's a repackaging of pre-digested ideas and facts that have been filtered of emotion for public consumption. What people really cherish are those unplanned moments—the authentic stuff that happens in live events.

Obviously, we're not suggesting that you weep and go to pieces on stage every time—it gets stale and even kind of creepy if you do this on a regular basis.

But most business idiots make the opposite mistake, rehearsing everything to the point where it becomes sterile. The words have been edited, censored, and approved at eight levels, and every slide has its own page of scripted notes. *Anyone* could give the presentation.

If you want to really connect with an audience, this should alarm you. If *anyone* could give the presentation, *no one* should give the presentation. It's filtered of *any* personality. There's nothing left to react to, and nowhere to insert a bit of *you*. Your audience feels left out.

BUT MY PRESENTATION IS TOTALLY BORING BEYOND BELIEF

If you plan to present something, try to make sure it's something you and your audience can get worked up about. Most business presentations aren't very involving, but you can make things much better if you keep in mind the following.

SCRIPT IT SO IT'S NOT SCRIPTED

Scripting your presentation is not a bad thing. In fact, we recommend it. The problem is when people read from their scripts *during* the presentation. The minute you lapse into words that sound like written English and not like spoken English, the audience knows you're reading. Instead, you should know your material *so* well that you have confidence deviating from it—to tell a story, to relate to an audience member, or to take some other detour.

Among the worst examples of scripting are those voice-mails that begin with the obligatory "This is an official firm communication going out to [insert 16 job titles here]. On behalf of the [insert two highest-ranking job titles here], I'd like to thank everyone for the tremendous excellence you've demonstrated in providing our world-class clients with benchmark service." We all know this is contrived and insincere bull that's being read from a page. The speaker clearly composed his thoughts before the audience came along, and we listeners know that he would have said the same thing no matter who showed up. Not completely rational on our part, but as human beings we all like to feel that the speaker is addressing us and not some generic seat warmer.

Scripting is good—but know your script, and then ad lib a bit—just don't read from it, or people will tune you out.

STORIES REPEL POLISH; USE THEM

If you're worried that your presentation is starting to sound canned or scripted, stories can help. Maybe you can't work yourself into a lather over the unfair scrapping of the old office carpet that held up extremely well for decades because, frankly, no one cares. No one cares about most business presentations. But a story about how the CFO's six-year-old niece ended up selecting the new carpet because she just got back from the zoo and likes zebras now—well, that could do the trick. More important, you and the audience can share a reaction to a story like that. When everyone reacts the same way to a story, a photo, music, or something else, that changes the way the audience listens and helps you connect. For more on stories, see Chapter 14, "An Actuary's Guide to Storytelling."

INTONATION

While there is a sort of "intonation" in writing—the "tone of voice"—the art of speaking is its own field. Of all the bad things that can happen to a business presenter, TelePrompTers are among the worst. They force a script on the presenter, control timing, and turn the speaker into a reader. The pace limits your ability to react, pause, or digress. Great speakers are immersed in what they are saying, and you know this through their intonation. Whether it's Churchill delivering a deadpan "We shall never surrender" or Reagan's "Mr. Gorbachev, tear down this wall," legendary political speeches are read from the heart—not from the monitor. Both speeches were prepared, but both speakers locked onto the lines that formed a channel between them and their audience. Dynamic business speakers, like Tom Peters, probably burn 800 calories during an hour-long presentation. Peters puts outrage on his side whenever he speaks, and the result is we all feel that we're watching a guru having a tantrum. This is fun. Sure, Tom Peters knows most or nearly all of what he wants to say in advance. But every time he makes a point, it's as though he's rediscovering that point and can't wait to deliver a (usually very informative) rant.

HIGHLIGHT THOSE FUMBLES

If you're not reading from your script, won't you make slips? Will people see you struggling a bit to come up with the perfect example? Absolutely, and they'll love (or at least like) you for it, because normal people struggle to put the right words together, laugh, and comment about things, and insert editorial comments all the time. We thrive on this. Go ahead and tell everyone what it feels like to have that microphone taped to your hairy chest—unless you're a woman, in which case you should say something different—or that you're going to need to reapply sunscreen if those stage lights get any brighter.

UMS AND AHS

Contrary to popular belief—and what speech coaches might advise—it is actually *OK* to allow a few natural "ums" and "ahs" into your speech. Don't force it, but let it happen. These are the natural bridges of human discourse—real words, used in every language to connect thoughts and fill pauses.

Speech pathologists call them "disfluencies"—and idiots worry that these words make them sound weak, nervous, or unprepared. But language research reveals them to be elegantly paced throughout normal speech, having a meaning that's subconsciously understood by the audience, as a pause, as time spent reconstructing a thought, or as a signal of the importance of an upcoming thought.

The International Sounds
of Humans Being, er, Human

English	ah, um, so, and, oh, like, you know, I mean
French	euh
Serbian/Croatian	ovay
Turkish	mmmmm
Hebrew	ehhh
Japanese	eto, ano
Spanish	este
Mandarin	neige, jeige
Dutch/German	uh, um, mmm
Swedish	eh, ah, aah, m, mm, hmm, ooh, a, oh
Norwegian	e, eh, m, hm

(Source: Erard, Michael, "Think Tank: Just Like, Er, Words, Not, Um, Throwaways," *New York Times,* Jan. 3, 2004.)

Idiots try hard to sound serious and polished, but in truth they would do much better being themselves, relaxing rather than editing their speech while trying to deliver it. It's not a bad thing to open the kimono in celebration of those "ums" and "ahs" for all the world to see.

BONDAGE

Bonding—now that we've got your attention for this final section—is one of the basics of getting your message across and succeeding as a speaker. People spend their lives looking for friends and lovers, hopefully more of the former. Parking your butt in a 90-minute slide show about the mission statement, or last year's numbers, rates somewhere far lower, unless the speaker can connect.

• • •

All of this doesn't mean that you should never rehearse. Check the room, make sure you know how to tie a necktie, don't stumble over your shoelaces—all of the usual mundane stuff in the usual presentation skills books is still important. Know your topic, know stories related to your topic, and know what gets your heart pumping about your topic. But never memorize your lines, prepare detailed cue cards or—heaven forbid—arrange for that TelePrompTer. Share your reactions. What was it about that topic that kept you awake all night? What would a cynic say about your message?

When the audience sees that you care enough to step out of that imaginary circle of rehearsed stuff and share something personal, they will care. If you take five seconds to reflect on something, or think of something new, your audience will more than forgive you.

They'll listen.

BEING FUNNY
IS SERIOUS BUSINESS

I've given my aides instructions that if trouble breaks out in any of the world's hot spots, they should wake me up immediately—even if I'm in a Cabinet meeting.

Things have been awfully busy at the White House lately. I've really been burning the mid-day oil.

It was easier to run for president when I was a boy. Back then there were only 13 states.

—RONALD REAGAN

LAUGHING WITH THE GIPPER

Over 50 films, eight years at the helm of California, eight years in the White House, victory in the Cold War, the Star Wars Defense Initiative, an outspoken and controversial wife, a public battle with his kids, a long and tragic decline with Alzheimer's disease—and what is Ronald Reagan remembered for? His humor.

On the occasion of Reagan's state funeral in June 2004, former president George H. W. Bush ("41") said of the GOP hero:

Perhaps as important as anything, I learned a lot about humor, a lot about laughter. And, oh, how President Reagan loved a good story. When asked, "How did your visit go with Bishop Tutu?" he replied, "So-so." It was typical. It was wonderful.

At the same funeral, former British prime minister Margaret Thatcher remembered the same trait in Reagan:

Yet his humour often had a purpose beyond humour. In the terrible hours after the attempt on his life, his easy jokes gave reassurance to an anxious world. They were evidence that in the aftermath of terror and in the midst of hysteria, one great heart at least remained sane and jocular. They were truly grace under pressure.

Humor, and everything it communicates—about lightness of spirit, about intention, about humility, about perspective—were hallmarks of Reagan's style. So that's politics. But is there any room for laughter at work?

BORING SCIENCE TAKES A LOOK AT HUMOR

Work is called "work," and not "fun," for a reason—it is actually "work," and no one would pay us to have "fun." But people who have studied laughter have found quantifiably positive effects. (Did you know that every time you have a good hearty laugh, you burn 3.5 calories?) (Did you ever wonder who pays researchers to come up with stuff like this?) Or that laughter releases the same endorphins you get from strenuous exercise? And it's not just good for your physical well-being; it's also good for your career.

Fabio Sala, of the consulting firm Hay/McBer, has re-

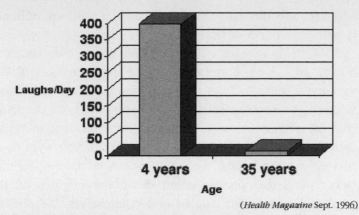

(*Health Magazine* Sept. 1996)

The average four-year-old laughs or smiles 400 times a day.
That number drops to 15 times a day by the time people reach 35.

searched humor extensively. In one study, he interviewed 60
executives from a major corporation and analyzed the inter-
viewees for their use of humor. He then cross-referenced the
executives' use of humor with three criteria: the performance
bonuses each received, how their peers ranked them, and
how they scored on aptitude tests. Sure enough, those who
used the most humor were also the ones who got the biggest
bonuses, were ranked higher by their peers, and aced the
tests.

Those ranked outstanding by their peers used humor more
than twice as often as average executives (17.8 times per hour
versus 7.5 times per hour). And their bonus sizes were directly
correlated with their use of humor.

People with a sense of humor rise through the ranks faster
and earn more money. It's a sign of self-confidence and security—a sign that you can afford a moment of levity, because
you don't have to hard-sell everyone on your talent. Humor
defuses conflict, reduces tension, and puts others at ease because sharing a laugh is a sign of friendship, not competition.
The bottom line: Humor makes us happy, makes people like

us more, and ultimately helps us connect with an audience (whether on paper or in person).

So with mountains of dull studies about the power of humor, why don't more people in the workplace use it? The stereotype we're sold, by the business media and suit manufacturers, is one of serious people in dark suits. It's the arms-crossed, smug-stare pose with the unwritten caption "I'm a capitalist. I'm brilliant, rich, and powerful." If you want to be successful and admired, we're told, you need to look like this. Never mind that people count down the minutes till the weekend so they can laugh and be themselves. We put our Saturday self on ice and take Mr. Grim to work all week. We're afraid that any kind of humor might have an impact on our credibility.

The answer is that it will—positively. You have to be good at what you do to laugh on the job. Whether it's a parody, some self-deprecation, or an amusing story, you're confident enough to take a risk and don't take yourself too seriously. Moreover, people want to listen to and believe messages coming from someone they *like*. And they *like* funny people.

I'M SO NOT FUNNY, IT'S NOT EVEN FUNNY

If you were Jerry Seinfeld or Jay Leno, you probably wouldn't be working with humorless business idiots. But you're not a career comedian, and humor's an art. We all know two people who could tell the same joke, and one of them would have us rolling on the floor while the other would get only solemn nods and a reflective "Gosh, I see." Timing, intonation, and our perception of the teller combine to leave us laughing our way to tears or wondering what we missed.

HUMOR GOES TO THE OFFICE

A lot of the hard-core jokes from the stand-up stage wouldn't play well at work, so the fact that you don't host one of the late-night shows isn't as important as you might think. There is a ton, maybe even a metric ton, of ways to inject humor into your personal brand. Most of them are subtle and easy. As with a lot of the brilliant and almost brilliant ideas we describe, the fact that no one else really seems to be trying works in your favor. You don't need to prepare a comedy routine to make things better. There are some things any of us can do to get people out of arms-crossed mode and get them interested in what we have to say.

SELF-DEPRECATION

The top reason people avoid humor at work is because it might offend someone, and this isn't a stupid reason. With every major religious, social, and racial group represented by lobbyists and lawyers, it can be expensive to offend someone, and companies spend a lot of time making sure this doesn't happen. Society is thin-skinned, as a rule, and it is fashionable to be oppressed. People actually aspire to victimhood, because it's a great way to retire young and well-off.

Aside from the only safe target—straight white men—you'll do well to exploit the one person you can be pretty sure won't sue you. And that would be *you*.

Self-deprecation is indispensable. The more successful you are, the better it works. If your executive vice president title is putting off your audience, cut yourself down to size. Was the forecast from last year completely wrong? Do a David Letterman–style Top 10 list of your worst predictions. Are you considered a technology junkie? Tell everyone you tried to beam your original presentation notes from your PC to your

PDA but think that they got stored in your Bluetooth wireless-enabled toaster oven by accident. Your printout is on a bagel in your hotel room.

Humor almost always brings some risk, but remember: It's always, *always* open season on yourself.

SATIRE AND PARODY

When it comes to presentations, business-as-usual is a slide deck with bullet points, charts, and graphs. If you want to connect, business-as-usual is a bad way to go. A bit of fun, on the other hand, goes a long way.

The beauty of satire and parody is that you can target something everyone hates. Think about expense reporting tools and performance appraisals. How difficult would it be to create a fictitious idiot and showcase the performance appraisal process using someone who spent the last year doing everything wrong? As long as the satire is relevant—that is, you're really trying to deliver a message about performance appraisals—it will help you make your point.

More important, it will make your point fun.

ANECDOTES

Storytelling is a key ally in the fight against the Tedium Trap (described in Part IV), but it's also indispensable when it comes to humor. Everyone gets a kick out of hearing about universal annoyances, such as the joys of airport security. Consumer-as-victim stories are usually winners as well, because we can all relate to bad experiences when buying a car, staying in a hotel, or getting ignored in a restaurant.

This is a fertile field because the world is full of morons who are generating story material faster than we can document it. You can reach into your own experience to find anecdotes, or relate a story you know from someone else's experience, or even track down collections of anecdotes involving the rich and famous. Try www.anecdotage.com.

THE SMALL AND UNEXPECTED

Humor is best when it isn't presented as "The Humor Segment"—part of something else that's big and boring. Nothing works better than small stuff done with a sense of mirth. Think about the mundane parts of work life: status report meetings, systems training, the appraisal process, e-mail auto-replies, and so on. Everyone expects them to be dull, and no one gives them much attention, but it doesn't take much to turn them into a source of amusement.

For example, what could be more mundane than the out-of-office auto-reply feature in e-mail? Instead of "Sonia will be out of the office from June 24 through June 27"—which people probably know anyway because you sent them an e-mail, a voicemail, and a calendar of the days you'd be gone—try something with a bit of charm: "Sonia will be out of the office June 24 through the 27th on a trip to the Amazon basin, where she and 98 other trained machete masters will be defending a primitive village that is under attack by aggressive giant mutant boas. Sonia will have access to e-mail, but will be checking only occasionally. Please use her mobile number only if your emergency is more serious than the snake thing."

The real charm is that it costs essentially nothing to do this. You'll get famous at work even though you're not at work, and everyone knows you're kidding. If someone doesn't figure out that you're kidding, then—bingo—the whole imagined trip goes directly into the community activities section of the corporate newsletter. Now that's legendary.

When we held a contest to gather jargon for the initial Bullfighter software release within our company, we could have called it the "Call for Jargon Contest" and offered a $100 gift certificate for dinner at some forgettable restaurant. But we called it the "Serious Bull Contest" and sent the winner to Bull-fighting school at the California Academy of Tauromaquia. We got more than 9,000 entries from 15,000 employees—unheard of at this (and probably any) firm. By breathing life into an inexpensive and outrageous idea, we created something that coaxed a smile out of just about everyone.

The mundane stuff will always be there. You might as well use it to make people smile.

ASIDES

OK, but I am affectionately known among colleagues as "Old Stoneface." No problem. Humor doesn't have to be a big production. From quotes to statistics to facts, there are countless ways to lighten things up.

Consider quotations. Oddball, seemingly unrelated quotes are a great way to flex your humor. Take a lyric from Mick Jagger, or an old Chinese proverb that rings true, and build your message around it. We use a quaint website called Cyber Nation. Its founders believe the dissemination of quotes will create a better world, and as of this writing, they provide a database of over 40,000 quotes for free. Whatever their motive, we like what they've done. Check out www.cyber-nation.com.

Anagrams and interesting or absurd facts (exactly how much did U.S. teenagers spend on navel piercing last year relative to our company's R&D expenditures?) can lighten up any presentation. Try the anagram tool at www.wordsmith.org, or the acronym generator at www.acronymfinder.com. All of this wonderful stuff is available, usually at no cost, which is about as much as it's worth anyway. Except, ahem, in the hands of a skilled humorist like you.

QUOTES 101

SITUATION	QUOTE
Need for Facts	Get your facts first, and then you can distort them as much as you please. *Mark Twain*
Evaluating Multiple Options	Of all the thirty-six alternatives, running away is best. *Chinese Proverb*
Need for Action	Talk doesn't cook rice. *Chinese Proverb*
Moving Forward	The only human institution which rejects progress is the cemetery. *Harold Wilson*
Taking a Chance, Risk	You'll always miss 100% of the shots you don't take. *Wayne Gretzky*
Leadership & Communication	When the eagles are silent, the parrots begin to jabber. *Winston Churchill*
Common Sense Solution	To see what is in front of one's nose requires a constant struggle. *George Orwell*
Competition	If you make every game a life and death proposition, you're going to have problems. For one thing, you'll be dead a lot. *Dean Smith*

LEAVE 'EM LAUGHING

If you want to break out of the Anonymity Trap, there's no greater ally than a bit of wit. Take this chapter as a starting point, and think about how you make people laugh outside of work. Are you the storyteller? The perpetual victim of bad customer service? The best celebrity impersonator? The closet playwright? An aspiring cartoonist? Renowned klutz? The worst golfer? The lazy one? The hyperactive one? The technophobe? What do your friends chide you for?

There is no one-size-fits-all approach to humor. Business idiots gave up trying a long time ago, and most of the corporate world is colorless and somber. As we've said more than a few times in these pages, this disaster is your opportunity.

If you want to connect with your audience, leave 'em laughing.

8

PICK UP
THE DAMN PHONE

You're sitting at work, chiseling away at a mountain of e-mails in a futile attempt to stay one step ahead of the next round of spam. All of a sudden, there's an alarming noise coming from that quaint little device sitting on your desk. You know, the one with the cord and handset. *Panic*. Good Lord, you think—what's that loud noise all about? Quickly you pull the manual down from the shelf and riffle through it. Right there, page 2: "The phone will ring when there's an incoming call." This could be one of those incoming call things! You lunge at the receiver, but too late. Dial tone. Of course—*the ringing noise*. Next time you'll be ready. Oh well, back to e-mail.

Whoever was trying to call you was probably selling mattresses or mortgages, but at least he got something right. In the deluge of e-mail, the telephone has reacquired a kind of novelty. The significant things that happen, that aren't face-to-face, happen live with the human voice. There's less economy in a phone call than an e-mail message, but economy isn't a good thing when you want to connect with people. People appreciate effort, and the opposite of effort is e-mail. That five-minute call requires that you dedicate five minutes of your time to the person you're calling. You talk. She listens. She talks. You listen. It's an amazing thing—to know someone's paying attention and to return the favor. Amazingly rare, anyway.

The voice is the ultimate weapon in the war on anonymity and the best way to create a relationship. If you have a tenuous relationship, if you exchange five e-mails without one live call, if you are dealing with an important issue, or if you are trying to persuade someone of something, invest a few minutes in a live call. On the phone, you have a better chance of hearing the truth, complete with all of those editorial comments and undertones that separate humans from business idiots. If you really want to know, pick up the damn phone.

CAN E-MAIL BE SAVED?

No.

CAN E-MAIL BE SAVED, PLEASE?

Oh, OK. We could argue that the technology behind e-mail is an evil conspiracy perpetrated by malevolent geeks set on monitoring all of our communications and then using our words to spam us with hundreds of inane ads, but frankly we haven't given that idea even a passing thought. E-mail *can* be the right choice. Business idiots have made it a minefield of dullness and obscurity, but for the brave ones—yes, you, sit up straight—it's possible to connect through e-mail if you keep a few things in mind.

1. ETIQUETTE

When the technology gods blessed us with e-mail, they couldn't banish all the evil from the garden. They created the Forward and CC: functions, and saw that these were pretty good. But under cover of darkness, those whose motives were impure corrupted the creation of the technology gods and added BCC: and, with a good dose of spite, Reply to All. The technology gods were hanging out at the beach on the seventh day discussing their stock options, so the great corruption went unnoticed. The effect of the BCC:/Reply-to-All curse was to make e-mail messages about as rare and valued as mosquitoes in Florida in the summer.

Copying the world on messages; hitting Reply to All to indicate your availability for a meeting when you need only reply to one; forwarding useless e-mails to score points; using the BCC feature to cover your . . . er, self—this behavior piles up and creates an exponential waste of time. Important messages become the exception, and smart colleagues who just don't want to deal with the mess tune it all out.

To counter it, every company should appoint an e-nanny. Give him (or her—a lot of guys won't sign up for a job with "nanny" in the title) an anonymous mailbox called "e-nanny," and keep the position secret. Rotate it every three months. Give e-nanny unlimited rein to skewer executives for empty, useless e-mail missives. Tell her to remind e-mail abusers of proper etiquette. Charge her with bringing the volume down, and the usefulness up.

2. GRABBER HEADLINES

We once received an e-mail message that began with "Are you about to delete this message?" Caught red-handed, we had no choice but to laugh and read it.

E-mail subject lines get a lot less attention than they de-

Subject Lines to Avoid

Re:

Re: re:

FW: Re: re: re:

Official Firm Communication

Important Official Firm Communication

FYI: Huge Attachment

Rules of the Road

FW: Your Opinion is Important

Message from General Counsel

---

serve. Magazine writers know that they have a title and possibly one or two sentences before the reader pays or leaves. That title earns them a check or gets them ignored. But business idiots ignore subject lines entirely. "Re:" followed by a bunch of blank spaces isn't much of a headline. It's better than "Re: re:" or "Re: re: re:"—but not by much. You can do better if you want people to bother to open your message.

Subject lines are your license to get creative. There is no law saying you have to be literal, and no harm done in having some humor. Tell a story in the body of your e-mail, choose a metaphor for your meeting, find a good quote—all of which takes about 10 minutes—and then find an intriguing subject line to go with it. Get creative to get read; otherwise, you risk getting zapped.

3. SUPPLY AND DEMAND

The law of supply and demand is always at work, and the hard truth of e-mail is that the supply is way too high. No one's awaiting your e-mails. (OK, maybe your mom.)

Still, too many people follow a strategy of one hundred percent communication via e-mail. Every time something happens, it's time for another stinkin' update cc'd to everyone. A similar problem is the consistent, once-a-month wrap-up of comings and goings. Or monthly "win" reports. These become more stuff everyone takes for granted and never bothers to read. The greatest improvement that can be made to these messages is to delete them prior to sending.

When you e-mail too much, nobody listens. And when you e-mail one thing regularly, nobody listens, either. If you don't believe us, read *The Rules*. It may be a dating book, but the same rules apply. E-mail is like dating: play hard to get. We've tried this and it works for us—we never go out with anyone.

Make your e-mails rare and valuable. Cut the supply, and they'll be in demand.

4. POWER OF THE PEN

Unless you're getting married, who writes letters or invitations by hand anymore?

Almost no one, but admit it: a handwritten—or even a typed but hand-signed—letter is something special. Who's worth a stamp anymore? What could be so important that it has to be printed on paper?

Obviously, it wouldn't make a lot of sense to trade e-mail for a new inkwell and quill. But what if the invitation to your next presentation went out on stationery instead of as a zipped up attachment to some anonymous e-mail? Maybe, at the end of the day, you hand-deliver those 20 or 40 invitations.

If the telephone is under attack by e-mail, the hand-signed letter is dead, was buried, and turned to dust a while ago. But whole books are made of correspondence between artists and lovers, and soldiers and spouses. Letters are the stuff of humanity. E-mail is the stuff of the recycle bin.

5. VARIETY IS THE SPICE OF E-MAIL

Ben Cohen of Ben and Jerry's knows how to make an electronic message stand out. He started True Majority, a lobbying group for left-leaning causes. To get people's attention, he

Let's say one cookie equals 10 billion dollars. The Pentagon's annual budget is forty cookies or *four hundred billion dollars* a year. So how much do you think we spend on this other stuff?

Not much. And that's why our schools don't work and children are left out in the cold. The government makes it sound like it's *impossible* to solve these problems, but it's not. Here's how we could do it . . .

Just take 5 cookies a year off this pile. Use 1 cookie to rebuild our schools, 1 to eliminate our need for Mideast oil, and 2 to feed all of the six million starving kids around the world. Then take the last cookie, (you've all done this before) and use half to provide health insurance and a quarter to provide Head Start for every kid that needs it. You can eat the other ¼ cookie. But remember, that's 2.5 billion dollars. Try not to choke!

Photo courtesy of True Majority ACTION and e-tractions

didn't write a doomed-to-fail memo pleading for funds. Instead, he created an animated short, describing the deficit in terms of Oreo cookies and sent it to a small group of people—who then forwarded it on to their friends, because it made fiscal policy accessible and easy to understand. More than 300,000 people signed up for more of what would have been spam, largely because they didn't want to miss one of these entertaining and informative animations.

Whether you use Oreos, animations, graphics, or 70-point red text, treat the reader of your message as someone who likes to be entertained. If e-mail is a poor substitute for a phone call, letter, or instant message, you can at least make your recipients feel as though they're getting a personal, handcrafted poor substitute.

III
The Hard-Sell Trap

Slimed

Uh-oh.

Here he comes. Maybe he's coming for someone else. Maybe I'm OK.

Maybe not. Dammit.

OK, stay calm. Think. Think.

[Mop sweat from brow. Throbbing in temple.]

That's what I get for stopping here.

The Hummer—hide behind that. It's right there—no! Oh, no. He saw me.

OK, I tried. I can handle this. Just calm down.

"Good afternoon, sir. Excuse me, sir? Sir! [Taps you on the shoulder.] *Hi! I'm Frank and that Hummer looks like your ticket to adventure.*"

"*Uh, hi.*"

It's all over. You've been slimed, and there's no way out. Your innocent Saturday-afternoon stroll around the local car lot to look at this year's fashions in taillights and grilles has been hijacked.

"Can I help you look at some cars today? What are you driving now? What do you do for a living? How much are you thinking about spending today? Do you have kids? Do you know Hummer drivers get twice the sex of other SUV owners? Off-road?" (Insert knowing wink here.)

Welcome to the hard sell, honed to perfection on used car

lots across the nation. Of course, the unwary seem to congregate in places like used car lots the way gnats seek out oncoming headlights, but you can be targeted almost anywhere—the department store, the dinner-time telemarketing call, even the corporate sales pitch.

"Buy now!"

"They call it an air cleaner, but I call it a miracle."

"We deliver best-in-class, value-added solutions that transform global enterprises into market leaders."

Audiences pick up on this bombast instantly, and they tune it out. Every product is a breakthrough, every deal is too good to pass up and will expire in 10 minutes, and all of those professional services will transform your company. Forget it. We've become immune to it. At the first sign of a sales job, we're looking for the exits.

This sounds obvious, but a few minutes spent flipping through any proposal or surfing a corporate Web page says otherwise. Business idiots spout the hard sell all day long. It's an obsession—how many *value-added*s and *empower*s can we stick on a page before someone from the state agriculture bureau stops by to confiscate the document for use as fertilizer? What would the product name actually look like without *world-class* in front of it? We may never know.

If you want to connect with your audience, keep in mind that people hate to be sold to, but they love to buy. Hard sell gets in the way and erodes trust. In the Anonymity Trap, we talked about how your personality and gift for being human can really help you connect with people, deliver your message, and become respected as a straight talker. Don't blow it by demoting yourself to a product spokesperson. You'll end up spending a lot of time speaking with the product.

Why does the hard sell live on when no one can stand it? After decades of infomercials, rigged stain-removal tests, and people jumping for joy at the sight of a new minivan parked in their driveway, does anyone buy this stuff? In the age of broadband, where the truth gets to anyone who wants it, the hard sell should be on the wane. But it's not, for a few reasons:

- **Fear.** It takes guts to start a discussion about a product or idea without wrapping it in superlatives. The last guy said his company's software was the world's leading value-driven enterprise solution. If I don't respond, won't everyone think his is better?
- **Habit.** We all know what to expect at a sales presentation or product demonstration, and professional salespeople have been using these since the dawn of capitalism. If a presentation doesn't start with 22 minutes of "why we're great," what else could we say for those 22 minutes?
- **Bad role models.** Unfortunately, there's ample evidence that infomercials and even traditional commercials generate sales. For some audiences, and in some situations, a blatant hard sell works. When it comes to bringing a human voice to the corporate world, though, it doesn't. The hard sell is an obstacle. Ultimately, that human voice is much more compelling.

The hard sell is communications cyanide—you're dead before starting. Like jargon and evasiveness, all of this hyperbole drives a wedge between you and any real people who happen to wander across your path. Respect your readers and your audience. Trust them with the facts, and treat them like people, or get out of their way.

9

THE NON-SELL SELL

You're sitting there in your La-Z-Boy recliner, Budweiser in hand, watching the Patriots trounce the Panthers, when the broadcasters announce they are cutting to a commercial. Four sponsorship logos and a slow-motion pan of the Gillette Stadium sign later, the game fades out and cuts to a man and a woman, relaxing in separate tubs, overlooking a seascape. (We're *always* finding ourselves in that situation.) You're not listening, because it's an ad. And it's another ad for erectile dysfunction, for crying out loud. The voiceover drones on about potential complications and side effects. Headache, upset stomach, nausea, blurred vision, dizziness, blah blah blah. And then, just as you're about to start channel surfing:

Men who experience an erection for more than four hours should seek immediate medical attention . . .

Four hours?! You look around for a pen. *Honey? Honey!* The nachos fall from your lap to the floor, but you don't care; you're still looking for that damn pen. *Finally.* And on your hand you write your ticket out of that middle-age crisis: C-I-A-L-I-S.

• • •

To date, this is the greatest example of the non-sell sell that we have ever found. The FDA requires that these side effect disclaimers get tacked on at the end of every pharmaceutical announcement. And usually, the reality of the disclaimer undoes whatever positive impact the ad may have had.

But not this time, baby. If you're going to need medical attention, this is the best reason you've heard.

The non-sell sell is persuasion in its most elegant form. It's fundamentally about letting people make up their own mind without the usual duress of the blaring hard sell. And the disclaimer at the end of the Cialis ad allows us to draw our own conclusion: this drug will turn me into the human version of the Washington Monument.

The more we try to declare, assert, and proclaim, the more our listeners suspect we are up to something. The cynical shield goes up, and instead of accepting what we are saying, they start to question it. But if we allow them to come to their own conclusions, we have a better chance of getting them on our side. People just seem to like an idea better when they think it's their own.

OK, BUT I HAVE SALES TARGETS TO MEET

The non-sell sell is *not* about surrendering the sale. (Believe us, we want you to meet your quota, because we actually need you to take this book all the way up to the cash register and then buy the sequel.) It is not about going wimpy and soft. It *is* about convincing, persuading, and cajoling by letting the sale happen naturally.

If you want to avoid the hard sell, you first have to get into the non-sell mindset. That's not always easy, because we've been raised on the hard sell. But we've found that once you start thinking about the non-sell, it becomes second nature. Here are some nuanced forms of selling without selling that should get you into that non-sell frame of mind.

HOW GREAT THOU ART—NOT

Here's a real excerpt from an e-mail sent to the employees of a large company after a nationwide meeting:

An Update on the All-Hands Meeting
from Our Roving Reporters

Putting on our journalist hats, the Project Springboard team hit the phones and email to conduct informal interviews after the October 17 All-Hands meeting. Why? To see what some of the thousands of people in 16 cities across the country thought about the day—was it a thumbs up or thumbs down? All in all, the day received a thumbs up. "We accomplished what we set out to accomplish," as one leader put it.

OK, let's see here. The people responsible for the meeting give themselves a grade and—brace yourself—it's a thumbs up. *Yeah, right.* No one believes this, even if it's absolutely true. As soon as the reader sees that "thumbs up" nonsense, brain alarms start going off: *Warning! Sensors detect incoming bullshit. Activate deflector shield. Disbelieve everything that follows.* Sure, it seems unfair, but the deluge of hard-sell manure that we have all been forced to wade through has made us extraordinarily sensitive to anything that remotely smacks of self-congratulation.

Self-congratulation is a particularly evil form of the hard sell. Not only does it fail to convince your audience, it often turns supporters and fence sitters into opponents and skeptics—a miracle transformation of the worst kind.

SHOW, DON'T TELL

In 2003, the film remake of *The Italian Job* was released. This high-speed caper flick, a remake of the 1969 classic, featured the beautiful Charlize Theron. Co-starring, and almost as beautiful, was a fleet of BMW Mini Coopers. Like Theron, the Minis were shown cavorting around Los Angeles doing all sorts of fun, daring maneuvers. The shots highlighted not only the performance of the Minis, but also their playful personality. In later research, BMW learned that sales increased 20 percent in markets where the film was shown.

Notice what the filmmakers didn't do: They didn't assert anything about the Mini. They didn't talk about dual-cone synchronizers, equal-length drive shaft, or four-sensor independent channel anti-lock brakes. They simply demonstrated. They let the car do the talking for them.

We all need to take a cue from *The Italian Job.* Demonstrate, don't assert.

ENOUGH ABOUT ME

Most people, when they want to persuade, immediately begin talking about "me." This works if you have a great anecdote that puts you on familiar terms with your audience. But if you really want to convince people of something they wouldn't otherwise know, think, or believe, you need to take yourself out of the equation

Take a hard look at the words "I" and "we" in your last brochure or speech.

The McKinsey Quarterly is an extremely successful marketing vehicle for McKinsey & Company. It positions the firm as the smartest, most experienced, most credible business advisors. But never does it talk about McKinsey's services. You won't find a "we" in there. This is part of McKinsey's prestige. It doesn't have to stoop to wrapping its services in superlatives the way many other consulting firms do. McKinsey is often regarded as the best because it doesn't take out any ads saying that it's the best. The company provides value, information, and education—and subscribers pay for it! Think about that: We actually pay McKinsey to get to read the company's marketing materials. Now that is classic.

This concept can also be applied on the personal level. Trying to get a new assignment? Pitch a piece of business? Land a job? Forget about going through the long list of your amazing qualifications. How about giving your perspective and point of view on the issues at hand? Start the conversation with "I've thought a lot about your issues and have some perspectives." Sure, this starts with "I," but it immediately shows that your focus is on the listener. Forcing yourself to talk this way will force you to *think* and *act differently* as well. If you put down the mirror and come with your mind firmly fixed on your audience, you will start preparing in a different way. You'll worry more about the other guy, and his issues and challenges.

THE ART OF SEDUCTION

If you're trying to woo an attractive date, you probably won't get far using a line like "Baby, I'm no Fred Flintstone, but I can sure make your Bedrock." (If this line works, let us know.) It's much the same in business. So why is it that we often bludgeon our audience with the obvious hard sell rather than practicing the art of subtlety?

We can't all produce overbearing infomercials, but the hard sell is alive and well even in the wasteland of creativity that is e-mail. Check the e-mail headers in your inbox, and count your bruises—bludgeoning is just a click away:

"Global Success Initiative Rollout Update"
"Legendary Places to Work Report"
"World Class IT Project conference call planned" (Woo hoo!
    Sign me up.)

It takes some serious willpower to actually open these, because we've already had our daily recommended allowance of condescending propaganda by the time we've finished reading the header. Pre-emptive deletion seems like the best move here. What kind of idiots named their own project the "success initiative"? Why are we calling ourselves "legendary"? Whatever was in these messages—and we really don't *care* what was in these messages—the senders could have done a lot more to pique our curiosity. So, in the cutthroat world of the modern inbox, these three are toast. Someone who had really wanted us to pounce on these messages might have used headers like these instead:

"Top Secret"
"We came in 14th" (Huh, wonder what that's about . . .)
"Dial in for the truth Wednesday"

Nothing dramatic, nothing deceptive, nothing in poor taste. Just short e-mail headers, small riddles that made us smile without launching into the old hard-sell song and dance. It doesn't take any longer to do this than it does to send out the usual pompous notice about the "Legendary Places to Work Report," but the difference in how the messages—and senders— are perceived is real.

Now take something as simple as the company newsletter. The title that's chosen sets the tone for the entire piece. Following are some real and noteworthy examples:

SEDUCTIVE	BLUDGEONING
"LUV Lines"	**"Building a Better Bank"**
Southwest Airlines	*TD Bank Financial Group*
"Miller Times"	**"Dixon on the Move"**
Miller Brewing Company	*Dixon Ticonderoga*
"The Whale Street Journal"	**"The CEO Success Report"**
Sea World San Diego	*Bizsuccess*

There are many ways to introduce the non-sell sell into your business communications. If you hit people over the head with the obvious, just like those lame pick-up lines, you're not likely to get too far. Seduce, don't bludgeon.

Hard Sell in Action: FAQs

Something bad has happened to one of the most potent accessories in the business communications arsenal: the Frequently Asked Question. This is troubling, because the *FAQ* acronym is legendary, a device revered for the value it ascribes to the reader's perspective.

When you write FAQs, this implies that you've thought about what the audience might ask. And readers are taking an enormous leap of faith, trusting you to be their agent, even though they know these "questions" were all made up. Still, readers aren't so naïve as to fall for FAQs that evade the truth and shovel the hard sell.

In the absence of any real hard science, we offer a taxonomy so you can rapidly classify those inane FAQs.

Category 1: Leading question masked as an FAQ

The most basic offense is the FAQ transformed into a leading question. Everyone can tell when an FAQ was constructed to sell an obscure feature or set up some kind of pre-packaged response that makes the responder look like some kind of genius. These bear no resemblance to any question anyone would ever have thought to ask:

- *Does our new ERM system allow me to view my dental plan in real time from my Bluetooth-capable wristwatch?*
- *How is the management of Nokia orientated: team Nokia or one-man show?*

Category 2: Propaganda masked as a FAQ

Sometimes when the hard sell is drenched in syrup, coated with chocolate sprinkles, and dusted with sugar, the only way to pass it off in public is to shove it into the once-honorable FAQ format. The supposed brilliance here is that even without an answer, we've built in all sorts of subliminal information:

- *If I enthusiastically embrace the new system, will it ensure a brighter future for the company and enable us to unleash our competitive strengths to focus on adding greater value for our customers?*
- *Arby's sounds like exactly the franchise I'm looking for and I like the quality and uniqueness of the food as well as the new building design. Whom do I call for more information?*

In this case, the person submitting the question is either *(a)* fictitious, or *(b)* someone who ought to call for a security escort when leaving the premises.

Category 3: The moron as questioner

When we read FAQs, we expect the writer to uphold our trust. We may not be the brightest thing on two legs, but the moment we suspect that the FAQs have been targeted at morons, we'll stop reading because we can't identify with these idiots:

- *What happens if we forget to plug our new Ultra-Slim laptop PCs into a wall outlet for, like, a month?*

We need to save the FAQ from this tide of corruption. This may be more than you ever wanted to know about the abuses of FAQs, but it was time to draw a line in the sand. Why? Because we have been asked about the decline of the FAQ. Frequently.

10

KICK THE HAPPY-
MESSENGER HABIT

There's also a more subtle form of the hard sell, and it's much harder to avoid. Think of it as hard sell's evil cousin.

It's human nature to want people to like you, and we go out of our way to make that happen. It helps you get a date for the prom, make friends, get into the right fraternity or sorority, get free air fresheners from the girl at the car wash, get the phone number of the girl at the car wash, go out with the girl at the car wash, find a better job, and generally do well in life so you can afford the kind of car that needs to be really clean all the time. We smile, tell jokes, and ask people how they are even if we don't actually care. But what we also do, more than anything, is dwell on the positive.

We're obsessed with delivering good news so we can bask in the halo. We distort or bend the truth to make it presentable. After business idiots have finished pouring maple syrup over everything, it's hard to tell that there was ever anything to worry about, except how to thank this charming presenter for explaining to us that everything is just boffo.

Accentuate the positive, and people will love you. Right? Not quite.

STOP TOSSING THE ROSE PETALS

Earlier, we talked about the gap between business communications and what everyone knows from e-mail, instant messenger, and casual conversation. In 1950, it might have been true that many workers didn't know the ugly truth. Since the grapevine went broadband, however, if there's bad news, you can bet that people know. The idea that anyone can conduct a business meeting by tossing rose petals from the podium and smiling a lot is worse than wrong—it destroys the presenter's credibility. Business idiots have precious little credibility left, so this is a bad move at best.

If you want to connect with your audience, this compulsion to accenutate the positive is your sworn enemy. Acknowledge and restate, honestly, what everyone knows anyway. People are used to having information spun, and they're ravenous for an occasional truth snack.

Quality has been down.
Our product has a design flaw.
There will be no bonuses this year.
Our sales force went out unprepared.
We lost a big customer because we couldn't deliver.
Next quarter will be rough because two of our patents expire.

These are all hypothetical, but they illustrate the point. If the real acknowledgment is couched in a lot of bull to make the bad news feel better, then your credibility suffers as people peel away the layers to figure out whether they can believe you. It may not always be true that everyone knows the unpleasant truth before you tell them, but it's a fool's bet to assume they won't learn soon. Not only that, but the bad news won't sting as long as you've given your colleagues the full story, and the respect they deserve.

BAD NEWS IS POWER: VIEW FROM THE BOTTOM

There aren't many leaders who can deliver bad news with candor. The ability to do this well confers a lot of prestige on the messenger. It demands courage, and immediately lets the audience know that you trust them enough to just say what needs to be said. You want them to know, and you're willing to show that you're human—whether you're worried or maybe partially at fault—by giving it to your listeners straight. People sit up and take notice of those who tell the truth. It's all about credibility.

Whatever comes next, after the bad news is on the table, has an eager audience. The power of that moment is unparalleled. You have complete credibility—the one who went into the ring with the truth and took the blows no one else would stand for.

Even if you're lucky enough to work somewhere where nothing really bad happens, there's always *some* truth that the business idiots have been shoving under the rug or burying on slide number 90. Don't be the happy messenger: find the truth. Pull it out, dust it off, and use it.

Remember, the glass is always half empty. Don't be afraid to spill it.

BAD NEWS IS TRUST—VIEW FROM THE TOP

It's one thing to spill the beans to those who work for us. But what about when we have to face up to the boss? When we're putting together that update, don't we all just nudge things a little to the upside? The pressure seems irresistible sometimes, because we don't want to embarrass ourselves or make enemies.

But think about it from your boss's perspective. All day long, every day of the year, she gets spun. And spun some more. Nobody wants to give her bad news, so usually nobody does. And if there is even a morsel of negativity out there, it gets run through the corporate Maytag until nearly all the real stuff is washed out.

And of course the opposite of spinning is whining—the person who is always delighted to report on some hypothetical catastrophe lurking in the corporate ozone. For the boss interested in reality, this isn't so helpful either.

So, if you are the boss, you probably turn on your trusty bullshit detector every time a subordinate comes to report to you. How refreshing it would be to have someone working for you who serves it up straight, time and again. Who's neither whiner nor spinner, but a reasoned truth teller.

DON'T BE SO NAÏVE

Back when the happy-messenger idea seemed like the way to go, life was easier. Stick that smile on your face, pick out the happy parts, and pack the rest into the appendix of the optional meeting pre-read. Delivering bad news, on the other hand, takes courage and intestinal fortitude, because we're no longer cheerleading.

There are two techniques you can use when you decide that bad news needs to be delivered:

1. DO SOMETHING

The old rule is to never present a problem without a solution. But there's an even better rule—never present a problem without actually *doing something* that represents a positive step to fix it. Even if it's nothing more than scheduling a trip to visit the disgruntled customer, do something. Show momentum toward an answer, even if you don't know what the answer is. There's a difference between bad news with signs of hope and bad news presented from the deepest pits of despair. You don't want to be the happy messenger, but it's not much better to be the hopeless prophet of doom.

2. PRONOUN POWER

To stay out of the world of spinners and whiners, make careful use of "I" and "we" and avoid using "them" or "they." If it's your responsibility, make it your problem. If you are even mildly connected to the problem, make it your problem. This is where "I" comes in handy. As soon as you start pointing fingers, the news goes from bad to ugly.

MR. MERNA

There is a job in the military called the CNO. Those called to accept that job may have the ultimate challenge in delivering bad news. *CNO* stands for "Casualty Notification Officer," and it is this officer's responsibility to track down and notify next of kin when a loved one has died in service.

Of course, the bad news that business people have to deliver is trivial in comparison with news of the death of a loved one. But sometimes when bad things happen in companies, lives can be disrupted and people can be hurt. We can take a lesson from the military on this kind of situation.

As you might suspect, the Department of Defense has a

Pronouns Behaving Badly

1. **"I am immensely proud of this achievement."**

   Makeover tip: Unless you just swam the English Channel with no help, after years of training by yourself and living alone, after your parents forbade you to do it and told you that you would definitely fail, find a way to use "we."

2. **"You have to resolve this quality issue for us to make our numbers."**

   Makeover tip: In this case, "you" is the fastest way to create defensiveness and make sure the other guy won't be interested in what you have to say. If you have *any* association with the issue, go for "we" instead.

3. **"We have faced these challenges and done great things."**

   Makeover tip: It's tempting to bask in the glow of success, but the legendary leader would probably go for "you" instead of "we." Deflect the credit, if you can do this without stretching the truth.

rather elaborate set of guidelines and scripts for CNOs to follow. But a former U.S. Marine CNO, Gerald F. Merna, wrote in a letter to *The Washington Post* about his experience:

> *Read the pamphlet . . . and then forget it, and rely on good old common sense and human instinct. Speak from the heart.*

Speak from the heart.
Well said, Mr. Merna.

11

FLOP PENANCE

A pril 14, 2004. The White House, East Room

THE PRESIDENT: John?

JOHN (Associated Press): *Thank you, Mr. President.*
  In the last campaign, you were asked a question about the biggest mistake you'd made in your life, and you used to like to joke that it was trading Sammy Sosa.

You've looked back before 9/11 for what mistakes might have been made. After 9/11, what would your biggest mistake be, would you say, and what lessons have you learned from it?

THE PRESIDENT: *I wish you'd have given me this written question ahead of time so I could plan for it.*

John, I'm sure historians will look back and say, gosh, he could've done it better this way or that way. You know, I just— I'm sure something will pop into my head here in the midst of this press conference, with all the pressure of trying to come up with an answer, but it hasn't yet.

I would've gone into Afghanistan the way we went into Afghanistan. Even knowing what I know today about the stockpiles of weapons, I still would've called upon the world to deal with Saddam Hussein . . .

I hope—I don't want to sound like I have made no mistakes. I'm confident I have. I just haven't—you just put me under the spot here, and maybe I'm not as quick on my feet as I should be in coming up with one.

Yes, Ann?

• • •

Love him or hate him, it's hard to deny that President Bush could have helped his cause at this press conference with even a slight admission of fallibility. What would it have hurt him to say "We could have done more; I wish that we had" or "Rebuilding Iraq is moving along smoothly, but it has been harder than we initially expected"?

Instead, he dodged the softball reporters had lobbed him and got hit with headlines like "Admit WMD Mistake, Survey Chief Tells Bush" shortly afterward.

In contrast, Richard Clarke, a former administration official, testified before the 9/11 commission and stunned the world with his forthright apology and personal acceptance of guilt.

Your government failed you . . . and I failed you. We tried hard, but that doesn't matter because we failed. And for that failure, I would ask . . . for your understanding and for your forgiveness.

Politics aside, this was remarkable. The families of 9/11 victims erupted in applause, and Clarke was widely praised for his strength of character in admitting a mistake.

GRADE INFLATION

For decades, business has cultivated a culture of denial. A few years ago, we had the unhappy experience of listening to the former CEO of a financial services firm, at the annual leadership meeting. While the company had suffered unprecedented losses, and the leaders would feel the pain in their collective wallets, the CEO did his absolute best to sidestep reality:

So, this has been an amazing year. What I like to call a perfect storm. Lots of obstacles. Huge barriers. An industry in turmoil. A lull in sales. Client dissatisfaction. Record-high turnover. And a painful decision to cut back salaries and lay off employees.

[Points to a slide showing a hurricane.]

But, I'm proud to say that we've weathered the storm quite well, and we're on our way to a healthy recovery. In terms of operational performance, I give us a B+. In terms of financial performance, a B–. And in terms of global capability, an A.

As you might expect, his speech went over like a poetry reading at a Guns 'N Roses concert. The audience was outraged. In the worst year in the history of his business this executive awarded himself two B's and an A. Around the room, everyone was trying to reconcile those inflated grades with their recently downsized wallets. But the CEO glossed over that—the single burning issue—with a medley of innocuous sound bites.

Had he gone hard on himself, he would have disarmed their frustration and might have brought them onto his side. The situation would still be challenging, but we can imagine that a listener in the audience might have had a different take on things. "What a crap year. Well, at least he gets it. Wonder what the plan is to get this train wreck back on track." Instead, the CEO further alienated them by refusing to even acknowledge a hint of failure on his part.

INSPIRATION FROM HOLLYWOOD?

Around Hollywood, a new trend seems to be emerging that business people should take note of. The term is "flop penance," coined by Adam Sternbergh in *The New York Times* (December 2003). When it became clear that they had a box-office disaster on their hands, Ben Affleck came out and confessed how poor his movie with fiancée Jennifer Lopez had turned out. On his promotional tour for *Gigli,* Affleck made no excuses:

> *It didn't work. We tried to fix it. But it was like putting a fish's tail on a donkey's head.*

Instead of enduring the ridicule resulting from a bunch of lame excuses, Hollywood has figured out that admitting an occasional failure isn't going to bring about the collapse of the film industry.

"I WAS DEAD WRONG"

How about flop penance in the business world? We could all take a lesson from legendary investor Warren Buffett of Berkshire Hathaway, who makes a habit of admitting his mistakes in plain English. In his 2002 letter to shareholders, Buffett wrote:

> *When I agreed in 1998 to merge Berkshire with Gen Re, I thought that company stuck to the three rules I've enumerated. I had studied the operation for decades and had observed underwriting discipline that was consistent and reserving that was conservative. At merger time, I detected no slippage in Gen Re's standards.*
>
> *I was dead wrong. Gen Re's culture and practices had substantially changed and unbeknownst to management—and to me—the company was grossly mispricing its current business. In addition, Gen Re had accumulated an aggregation of risks that would have been fatal had, say, terrorists detonated several large-scale nuclear bombs in an attack on the U.S. A disaster of that scope was highly improbable, of course, but it is up to insurers to limit their risks in a manner that leaves their finances rock-solid if the "impossible" happens. Indeed, had Gen Re remained independent, the World Trade Center attack alone would have threatened the company's existence.*

"I was dead wrong." He has no problem recognizing his own successes and his own failures. We respect this. We *trust* him. He comes across competent and confident. In fact, this humility is the hallmark of great business leaders.

OK, BUT I'M A FEW CLAMS SHORT
OF A BILLION . . .

Sure, if you're like Warren Buffett and have more money than God, you can probably afford to admit some mistakes now and then. But what about those of us who haven't quite made it to Buffett's fame or tax bracket?

In many ways, the higher you rise, the harder this gets. That's because when you reach the rarefied air in the upper echelons of the organization chart, you will have lots of handlers who will advise you otherwise. Attorneys, PR flacks, HR wonks, and personal coaches will all spin, shape, contour, and beat your admission into submission. And it won't come out looking anything like the mea culpa that was intended.

For those of us whose main concerns aren't the price of jet fuel or what to tip the chauffeur at Christmas, it may seem as if there's a lot to lose by airing your missteps in public. But as long as you don't overdo it—if the "Screw-Up of the Day" becomes a running feature of the daily status meeting, you might want to think about giving the confession thing a rest—there's far more to gain.

That's because promoting an aura of perfection and invincibility actually works *against* you. It's a huge rapport builder to show that you wrestled with a decision, had some doubts, put some thought into it, and had the fortitude to admit that you made the wrong decision. Or missed the deadline. Or handled the negotiations poorly. It happens, and people know it happens. If you pretend it never happens, you're not doing yourself a favor.

This is the non-sell payoff. If accentuating the positive makes the negative even worse, then the converse is also true: accentuating the negative makes the positive even better.

Apologizing for Profit

At some medical schools, including Vanderbilt University School of Medicine in Nashville, Tennessee, courses in communicating errors and apologizing are now mandatory for medical students and residents. Insurers across the nation, including General Electric's giant Medical Protective unit, are beginning to urge their clients to acknowledge errors and apologize.

Nothing is more effective in reducing liability than "an authentically offered apology," says Colorado surgeon Michael Woods, who teaches seminars for doctors and malpractice insurers on the importance of apologizing.

Rachel Zimmerman, "Doctors' New Tool to Fight Lawsuits: Saying 'I'm Sorry,' " *Wall Street Journal,* May 18, 2004.

When you are at fault, the harder you go on yourself, the easier others will go on you. Put your ego down for its midafternoon nap and admit some fault. Your audience's capacity for forgiveness is almost as great as their distaste for denial. Use it to your advantage.

A ROSE BY ANY OTHER NAME

Former Major League baseball slugger Pete Rose confessed to betting on the sport only after it became clear to him that a confession was his only chance to get into the Baseball Hall of Fame. Even then, he couldn't quite bring himself to the point of really showing remorse. In his book, *My Prison Without Bars,* Rose says: "I'm sure that I'm supposed to act all sorry or sad or guilty now that I've accepted that I've done something wrong. But you see, I'm just not built that way."

What Rose lacked in his confession was *authenticity.* Compare that to how Johnson & Johnson executives reacted when Tylenol was found poisoned in the early 1980s. *The Washington Post* noted, "What Johnson & Johnson executives have done is communicate the message that the company is candid, contrite, compassionate, committed to solving the murders and protecting the public." Then Johnson & Johnson displayed another element of the effective apology—specific, tangible, action steps to fix the problem. Their immediate, massive recall of 31 million bottles at a cost of over $100 million, the cessation of all production, and the quick introduction of a tamper-resistant substitute sent a clear signal that they were genuinely committed to righting the wrong.

Authenticity, promptness, and clear action are the stuff that effective apologies are made of. We're not suggesting you drop to the floor, do 10 Hail Marys, and confess all your flaws and shortcomings before the boss. But pretending that everything is hunky-dory and constructing an elaborate veneer of perfection when you've made an obvious error will only fuel the fire. Business people who live by denial appear ignorant, egotistical, and dishonest. Whether with your wife, your client, a customer, or a colleague—a little fessing up goes a long way.

You can take this one to the bank: The harder you go on yourself, the easier others will go on you.

The Art of the Apology

Sharon Elison, a communications consultant and author, has described three forms of apologies that really aren't. Elison's categories are an excellent field guide to bull-spotting among the several species of would-be apologies.

The Excuse: "I'm sorry I didn't deliver the report. I had a lot of last-minute fires to fight."

Translation: Yes, it happened, but it wasn't really my fault because of other stuff that happened to me. (Conveniently, that other stuff is someone else's fault, so the result here is to transfer the blame.)

Denial of Intent: "I'm sorry I didn't deliver the report. I had wanted to get it done a week before our meeting."

Translation: The reluctant apologist here tries to join the other side by pointing out her good intentions and thereby putting herself in a sympathetic light. This is a subtle way of turning herself into a victim to avoid taking the blame.

Blame: "I'm sorry I didn't deliver that report. Was the department not able to run smoothly in the absence of one report?"

Translation: Arguably the worst sort of non-apology, the blame technique trivializes whatever required an apology by throwing the problem back in the faces of the larger group. "The real reason I screwed up was because everything else around me is done wrong. My mistake isn't even worth mentioning." Uh . . . sure.

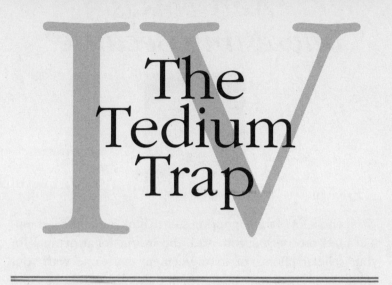

IV
The Tedium Trap

A healthy male adult bore consumes each year one and a half times his own weight in other people's patience.

—JOHN UPDIKE

And This Is Interesting Because?

We spend a lot of time ignoring stuff. Think about the last mutual fund prospectus you read, the instructional manual for your cellular phone, or the agreement that came with your credit card. There may be things in there that would be good to know, but no one in her right mind is going to slog through the fine print on the off chance there's something relevant or intriguing.

Business idiots spend their lives delivering the fine print to audiences who don't really care. Sometimes the message is timely and smart, sometimes it's the usual bull, but whatever—they assume the audience exists to take notes.

In real life, though, the audience *isn't* there to take notes. We're continually surfing our environment for something cool. A story that gets to us, a lively debate, a brilliant insight, a subject that we can't resist. Everything else—even if it's something as wonderful as a slide showing a company's complete organizational chart in a 2-point font—is meaningless noise. We can always look it up later if it matters, and based on our experience, it doesn't.

In real life, we walk into every meeting and open every book with the hope that some kind of entertainment will be mixed in with the factual stuff. The more we expect a dull up-date, the more we crave entertainment. *Is the presenter like me? I wonder if he'll throw one of those tantrums—that would be cool. Boy, we got our asses kicked on that subcontracting deal—I'll bet she hides that whole deal in the closet. Look at that tan—maybe he just got back from someplace nice. What's up with the splint on her hand?*

If all of this doesn't sound like a close fit with your presen-tation outline, it's time to put away the outline. A big chunk of the real agenda lives in your audience's heads. To connect with them, you need to get a copy of that part of the agenda and tell your part of the story in a way that people will be talk-ing about long after you're done with that meeting. It might be a corporate legend that says it all in a short story, an on-the-cheap video you've made that makes your point vivid, or sim-ply your inimitable style.

We've talked about how obscurity, anonymity, and the hard sell prevent you from connecting with an audience. The Te-dium Trap is about *entertainment*. There are too many nice people with clear messages who fade into the din of business with no real impact because they didn't realize they were in show business. Whether it's writing or speaking, you're an en-tertainer. (If you're great at it, maybe the tabloids will start to chase you someday. Ah, dreams.)

The reality is that business is usually boring. Your job is to translate it into relevant stories and personal commentary—that's the stuff life is made of. This isn't always easy. But the silver lining is that business idiots have lowered the bar so much, you really don't need a shelf full of Academy Awards to escape the Tedium Trap.

12

SEX, DRUGS, AND ROCK 'N' ROLL FOR BUSINESS PEOPLE

Let's face it, if you charged $110 for a ticket to the next sales meeting, attendance would be, well, down. No one wants to go to these things. They're a bore. All the charts look the same, the numbers are still dripping with baby oil from a couple of weeks spent on the massage table, and if it's like last month's meeting, there will be no music, dancing, or naked people. Maybe some muffins and coffee.

For you, boredom is a sworn foe. If something doesn't create a sense of curiosity or spark intrigue, it loses relevance for the audience. They seek arousal elsewhere, like their Black-Berry, or the piece of lint threatening to mount an attack on the person in front of them. Show me something fun, something interesting. *Now.* It's the voice that has followed us around since we were six when it said "This toy sucks. I need a new one."

If you want to connect with an audience, you have to get

their attention. Make it relevant. Make it vivid. Make it compelling. Whether you like it or not, you're in the entertainment business. If you don't find a way to keep their attention, someone or something else will. Sex, movies, toys, sex toys, movies about sex, movies about toys, whatever. The mind is always on the prowl.

But there's hope. You don't have to be Steven Spielberg to be entertaining and engaging.

LEGENDARY AND NAKED

Back in Chapter 2, we talked about words to stay away from—jargon and other incomprehensible words that obscure, rather than clarify, your meaning. In addition to the all-important Delete key, there are words that can help. If you do an Internet search for "power words," you'll get something like "The Life Insurance Agents Amazing & Sensational List of Power Words." These may help you move a lot of variable annuities, but they're decidedly *not* the words you are looking for.

Intriguing words are like interns to presidents—they bait you. They're a signal that someone has actually created an original presentation or written an original introduction—because we *know* none of those dull slides that have been circulating for the last two years ever said anything about "naked" or "flummoxed." We've included a starter list for you, but be sure to build your own list.

JUST THE FACTS, MA'AM

When it comes to relevance, facts trump generalizations. Business idiots love generalizations, because somehow these broad assertions have become the sign of your stature. If you

Starter List of Intriguing Words

beast	pandemonium	abracadabra
nonsense	serendipity	whopper
lumpy	zombie	annihilate
wimpy	suicidal	turbocharged
thunderous	monolithic	rare
hyperactive	naked	romp
maniacal	sizzling	nauseous
sweaty	weird	phantom
toxic	fugitive	paralyze
cryptic	maladroit	sloppy
tainted	mind-boggling	frenzy
blasphemous	insane	iridescent
flummox	lollapalooza	cataclysmic
wizard	nasty	Monica
staccato	gargantuan	squeamish

know everything, it's easy to generalize. If you know next to nothing, you can always come up with a sweeping statement about something.

Here's a real excerpt from a real Fortune 500 CEO's message to the entire organization:

> *We continue to be recognized as one of the best places to work in America. Our human resources programs are being copied by others for their innovation and effectiveness.*

Yeah, right.

Now here's the rub—what the executive was saying was true. This company *is* an HR leader. But how do you think this message was received? It probably wasn't. Instead, he should have demonstrated how this is true. Not through a boring recitation of mind-numbing statistics, but with a couple of stories that make the point. If the company was truly recognized as one of the best places to work, there have to be some data to prove this. Third parties must have recognized the company. Internal surveys must reinforce it. If other companies are copying us, who are they? How do we know? Somewhere, somehow, the data must exist—otherwise the assertion is bogus.

Back up the assertion with something real and tangible, or don't bother making it.

BRING IT TO LIFE

We were giving a speech to a group of technology marketing executives about a new movement in marketing called

ASSERTION	FACT
Many leading companies are offshoring work to low-cost locations.	Forty-seven companies on Fortune's 100 Best Places to Work are offshoring work to low-cost locations.
Traffic in large American cities has become a serious, expensive problem.	In Los Angeles, motorists spend 82 hours each year in gridlock.
Product design at our company is a bigger issue than customer service.	Of 244 returns this month, 197 were for the X500 wireless modem.

"branded content." Branded content (OK, wake me up in an hour) is about demonstrating value, instead of asserting it. Most commercials scream "We're the best!! Buy now!!" to an audience immune to the hard-sell-as-usual. We knew branded content was better than the "Buy Now!!" approach, but how do you make that relevant to a bunch of technology marketers?

We used the 2003 remake of the movie *The Italian Job* as an example. The movie was essentially one giant commercial for BMW's Mini Cooper. Kind of interesting, because after an hour and a half, the endearing little cars become co-stars in a fast-paced caper flick.

But after a few minutes of searching the Web, we learned that:

1. They used 33 Minis during the filming.
2. Sales increased 20 percent in markets where the movie was showing.

Presto! A pretty good anecdotal example became a compelling example with just a couple of small details. Cool example, concrete numbers, and a memorable result. Research cost: free.

AROUSE YOUR FRIENDS AND CO-WORKERS

Real people in real life are not politically correct. They have body parts, and acknowledge them. They recognize that men and women have wonderful and mysterious differences, and they acknowledge them. They listen, without guilt, to music by artists who have more raps on their criminal file than in their songs. They understand that certain cultures and ethnicities have amazing and sometimes curious inclinations, and they talk about them. They tell jokes that are not lily white. Occasionally, they swear. And, yes, they have sex.

But the human resources storm troopers have won. Today, we have to be so careful and cautious about being politically correct that we might as well have a straitjacket on—our mouths and our pens. The censorship starts with things as provocative as the common matzoh ball.

As one of the unsuspecting masses, you might have thought that a matzoh ball is basically a lump of matzoh meal, shaped into a sphere and dumped into chicken broth. According to the HR team at one company, however, you would be mistaken. It could actually be taken as an anti-Semitic symbol. In a welcome column in one of the company's internal newsletters, a New York–based editor referred to his mom's matzoh ball soup recipe. The sages in HR immediately demanded an explanation of what a matzoh ball was. Upon being told this privileged information, they escalated the newsletter review to the executive level and ruled that the offending reference be removed lest those of Jewish faith be offended. All of this after three Jewish people—the writer of the editorial, the regional editor, and the editor-in-chief—had had a good laugh at the original piece.

When it comes to the mention of anything related to sex, reality gets even more of a cold shoulder. This straitjacket makes people a lot less interesting and entertaining. Ironically, this hypersensitivity to workplace PC behavior creates an opportunity for aspiring leaders to show that they're human, just like their audience, all while having a little fun and bringing some entertainment into the workplace. Not only will that make you more effective, but your shackled soul will thank you for the taste of liberty you have provided.

So, how do you do this without being labeled a boor? Be subtle and be considerate. Use subjects and words and concepts that are generally considered off-limits, but remove yourself one step from what really is off-limits. Be acceptably naughty.

Let's start with S-E-X. You can pretty much be assured that 99.9 percent of your audience will find S-E-X (pulse rising?) infinitely more interesting than the latest bulletin from the Financial Accounting Standards Board. Moreover, they're already thinking about it. If you want everyone to think you're clairvoyant, bring S-E-X into the discussion.

Want to make a riveting presentation on advertising and product image? Feature those performance enhancement glamour drugs—Viagra, Levitra, and whatever comes next, or last, or whatever. You know what we mean. Right. Anyhow, they're real products, and the economics and marketing considerations are just as relevant as boring stuff like paper towel holders, garbage disposals, and kids' scooters.

But guaranteed, your audience will perk up. They will pay attention because you have just done the unmentionable. You have actually alluded to sex and confessed that you have the same thing on your mind as half of your audience. Not surprisingly, you've connected with your audience, and without offending anyone. That's the power of S-E-X.

I SWEAR, YOU SHOULD

Mark Twain wrote, "Under certain circumstances profanity provides a relief denied even to prayer."

We're not advocating more profanity in the workplace, because there's entirely too much now. But in selected situations, you really can swear *a little*. Real people say these words and think them constantly. Your audience has these words in that top 100 list of words so innate that you're almost sharing their thoughts when you express yourself this way.

Forget the harsh and offensive stuff. You can say words like *damn, screwed-up, bull,* and *crap,* in the right context. Try it now. Close your eyes, open your mouth and say "crap." Now visualize yourself in a business meeting saying "crap." Now go one step further—put it in writing:

To move forward effectively, we will need to cut the crap and tackle issues head on!

You devil, you.

EMBARRASSING AND ANNOYING

Here are some special tips: Celebrate annoyance and seek out embarrassment (just think—you actually paid for this advice).

It's all about letting your audience know that you belong to the same species they do. The annoying things that nobody likes to mention are actually the things that everyone loves to hear about. The Official List of Annoying Stuff is endless, even if you limit it to airlines, downtown parking laws, and how to reset the clock in your German car. And those common little embarrassments that seem off-limits are actually very much on target when it comes to connecting. Here are a couple of examples:

Spam—What's more annoying than opening your inbox and finding it full of ads for male enhancement drugs? You can use this as a reference to not wanting to overload people with useless information or work, like spam you get "to lower your mortgage and enlarge your body parts." People will pay attention, and they will appreciate your allusion to something supposedly off-limits. A common annoyance is one of those safe topics that brings you closer to your audience, and there's no better target than something everyone hates.

AA—Say you want to address a difficult issue your organization is facing. Start off with a slide showing the Alcoholics Anonymous famous 12-step addiction-recovery program. Of course, step one is admitting you have a problem. You will have people's attention. Relating Alcoholics Anonymous to business issues is strange and unexpected and, of course, officially off-limits. But not really—unless you demean the program or trivialize someone's problem with alcoholism. Mere mention is enough to show that there's a compelling strategy to how you organized your presentation. It will make your point, and it (and you) will be remembered.

So here's the key idea: Next time your instincts tell you that a reference or topic is really good to use, but is off-limits because it is politically incorrect, think a second time. First, it probably is OK. You may be suffering from superparanoid conditioning at the hands of the PC police. Second—and this really is important—make sure your use of the topic is one or two steps removed from stuff that is actually off-limits.

VISUAL METAPHOR MAKEOVERS

Subtlety can be the difference between good communicators and great ones. Most business people think their goal is to get people to pay attention. Not bad, but not good enough. Great communicators get people to *think*.

Pictures are a good place to start, and many business people have the right intention. A picture is worth a thousand words. The problem is, way too many are insipid, boring, and stupid. A common culprit for business presentations is stock clip art. It's so easy—search, click, insert. Thousands and thousands of standard pictures to make just about any point you want. But most clip art is so obvious and pedantic that it just begs to be ignored. Who creates this stuff anyway?

But don't give up on pictures. Pictures can be extremely powerful metaphors for making your point. Watch audiences during a presentation perk up when an interesting picture is shown.

Next time, try something different. Add a little abstraction to your pictures. Look for the less obvious pictures that tell more of a story or use a twist of humor to get people's attention. Make them stop, pause, and consider. Maybe even smile.

Business Situation	Cheesy Clip Art	Makeover
We've taken on more than we can handle		
We're behind schedule		
The situation is deteriorating		

Left column © 2004 Microsoft Corp. Lucy photo Hulton Archive/CBS Photo Archive/Getty Images

We included a few examples on p. 131. The makeovers are real examples used in management presentations in a big humongous accounting and consulting firm. So don't try to tell us that your company is too conservative for this—we've kept the navy suit and white shirt industries in business for decades, maybe longer.

The key thing about these metaphors is something we call "obvious subtlety." Lucy and Ethel in the chocolate factory is a classic television skit and an obvious allusion to a situation where one is in over her head. But the brain has to work a bit (not much) to relate it to the business situation at hand—there is the subtlety. *OK, Lucy and Ethel. We have more work than we can handle. Eureka—puzzle solved! (Insert smile here.)* The key is to give the audience something to work out for themselves. And don't give them the Sunday *New York Times* crossword—it needs to be obvious, or made obvious with a simple statement. Contrast that with the clip art with loads of work piled up on the desk. *Yeah, too much work—duh. Tell me something I don't know.*

SLIGHTLY NAUGHTY

If you want to see a bunch of kids have a bad time in an ice cream shop, take them to the place that serves only vanilla. Generalizations are the vanilla of the business world, and business idiots are serving up scoop upon scoop. It's enough to make your teeth hurt.

Your goal is to create a rapport with an audience, to show them that your thoughts aren't so different from theirs. You have the same preoccupations, annoyances, and reactions to life that they do, and you care enough to entertain them. You're mint chocolate chip.

If you listen closely to a talented comedian—one whose whole routine isn't X-rated—you'll hear a lot of observations about things like air travel, blind dates, speeding tickets, bad restaurant service, and hangovers. *The specifics make the routine engaging,* even if we all know that air travel is a huge inconvenience and that blind dates are—well, the odds aren't what we sometimes would like to believe. A speeding ticket isn't exactly going to bring *The New York Times* around to interview you, but talking about your run-in with the law will captivate. Naughty? Slightly, and that's perfect.

Now, combine the blind date, air travel, and the speeding ticket with a run-in with the law. You're onto something. Call Spielberg. If he's not interested, you can always go back to that F-A-S-B presentation.

13

MAKE YOUR POINT
BY MAKING THEIRS

It's midnight. You're safely ensconced in your suite at the Courtyard Inn. The TV's flickering in the background. It's Clint Eastwood week on the Superstation—there's a lot of dust, a few ambushes, a lot of bullets, and not a lot of dialogue. The extra little hotel soaps are safely packed away in the side pocket of your suitcase. You have already raided the minibar for the Famous Amos chocolate chip cookies and, with your personal trainer in some other city, are now trying to decide on dessert.

You're on the agenda at 8:00 A.M. tomorrow. So what are you worried about?

If you've been hanging out with business idiots, probably all the wrong things—like making sure your PowerPoint bullet points are perfectly lined up and that you've memorized all eight words in your new job title.

What you should be worried about is what your audience is worried about. One of the biggest reasons business people speak like idiots is that they spend way too much time talking about what's in their head and not nearly enough time on what might be floating around in the minds of their audience.

To your audience, everything you say is irrelevant until it touches on something they care about. Avoiding the Tedium Trap is fundamentally about leaving the cocoon of your skull and crawling into theirs. And the most important part of doing this is to understand and deal with their issues and objections.

Sometimes this is obvious. The guys on the board of the White Star Line had some obvious things to go over during the meeting after the *Titanic* sank. But even if your agenda is more mundane, the important thing is that the agenda isn't just a collection of all the things on your mind. The first step to avoiding the Tedium Trap is to get the really important stuff on the agenda, and "really important" is always in the eyes of the audience.

Make your point by making theirs.

THE STATISTICALLY INVALID SURVEY

Let's say you need to make a pitch, address an audience, facil-itate a meeting—whatever the situation. Instead of spell-checking your document for the forty-seventh time, try talking to a few audience members. You don't need to speak to a lot of people—usually just a couple or a handful. Ask them what they want to see addressed in the meeting or presentation. Ask them what concerns or questions they have. Ask them what they don't want to hear.

Ask them whether they were watching Clint Eastwood on the Superstation last night.

Just ask them stuff.

Then, when you start the session, allude to your conversations. Tell the audience that you took the opportunity to talk to some of them beforehand. And then repeat or paraphrase what they said. This always goes a long, long way. First, you may actually learn something that you didn't know before. Also, the gesture of reaching out will immediately connect you to your audience. You will have their attention because, surprise, you are actually talking about something that *they* are interested in—as in *themselves*. Funny how that works.

DISARMAMENT

If you've ever bought a house, you know the drill. You go in and look around. The bedrooms are so small that even Stuart Little would feel cramped. But the real estate agent is expertly trained, so when you finally muster the courage say you are a little worried about adult-onset claustrophobia, she's ready because she is well versed in the fine art of handling objections.

While you're worrying about those above-ground coffins, she's talking "cozy" and "intimate." Sure, they may look small, but they really live large.

Conventional wisdom calls for you to think through all the issues and concerns someone might bring up. And prepare answers for them. When the issues come up, you (and the agent selling the Stuart Little residence) are ready with the instant prepackaged response.

Conventional wisdom ignores a fundamental truth: Most objections never get aired. They sit there, marinating in someone's head like bad beef teriyaki, and when you don't address them, the cynics of the world (all 6.3 billion of us) have their concerns reinforced.

I knew it!
He's afraid to bring it up.
Wow, must be bad.
Even worse than I thought.

It's hard for people to focus on what you are trying to convey until you scratch their itch.

The answer is disarmament. Don't wait for your audience to air those issues and then swat them away like an annoying swarm of gnats. Those objections matter. In fact, to your audience, they may be the only agenda items. Is there anything worse than the brush-off? Well, yes. Let those objections simmer unattended while you take an oblivious stroll down your own private promenade.

How about starting off your discussion with the issues? Or with the problems with your proposal? Or with the controver-

---

Furrowed-Brow Syndrome

What do you do if you're in the middle of a discussion or presentation and you see a colleague across the table with a twist of skepticism on his face, his arms tightly folded across his chest, displaying an almost involuntary horizontal shaking of the head? Try this: "Joe (the one who is scowling), looks like you have a furrowed brow. Is there something you disagree with or something I'm not explaining very well?" Just like in twisting those rabbit ears on your television set—you remember those, right?—reception picks up. The whole audience appreciates the fact that you're aware enough to know that things aren't going so well. Major points for that. Courage for calling it out. More points. A break in the routine. More points. Keep scoring.

---

sies inherent in it? Or some things you would change if you had more time? At a minimum, start by saying "There are some things that we just haven't figured out about this yet." Don't fall into a timid, dump-on-yourself, confidence-destroying opening. It takes a ton of confidence to get the objections out and deal with them.

WE HAVE MET THE ENEMY AND SLEPT IN HIS UNIFORM

If there is a controversial issue that needs to be addressed—and when isn't there one?—start by presenting both sides of the issue, regardless of which side you are on. The key is to be super-diligent about preparing the opposing side. If you want option A, it's not enough to toss out a few feeble arguments for option B. Be schizophrenic—this will be easy for some of us. Don't be dismissive—ever. Put yourself on the side of the option B team and argue it as if you mean it, in your best authentic style.

This double argument is crucial. *People don't listen well until they feel like they have nothing to say.* If the option B team sees that you've listened to their point of view, taken it seriously, and argued it as though it were your view, they're less likely to cross their arms and shake their heads during your otherwise riveting presentation.

All parties feel as if they have been heard and are much better prepared to hear you and understand your point of view. Dr. Phil would be proud.

SNAKES, DYSLEXIA, AND ACCOUNTING STANDARDS

The best movie heroes have their wrinkles. George Lucas's swashbuckling archaeologist, Indiana Jones, rescued the Ark of the Covenant from the Nazi hordes, conquered evil cults, overcame grisly traps in ancient tombs, and came through it all with about the same amount of bruising we get moving stuff to clean the garage.

But Lucas and director Steven Spielberg wanted to make us like Indiana Jones, so he made him human. For all of his heroics, the legendary Dr. Jones was petrified of snakes. That comes out in the *first scene*.

The lesson: Show your humanity, and your audience will feel that they know you better. Suddenly, you're relevant. Even if your presentation consists of a complete reading of the U.S. tax code set to Brahms, someone will feel bad about ignoring you because you suddenly seem more like a real person than one of those cardboard clones delivering the usual pre-digested messages.

One way to reveal your humanity is to reveal a weakness. Exposing a weakness builds trust and solidarity. It underscores a person's authenticity.

Richard Branson, the brilliant founder of the Virgin brands, has a talent for communicating his fraility. He readily admits to his dyslexia and is generally ill at ease when interviewed in public. For all of his success and wealth, here's a guy who has some things he wrestles with—the kinds of things we associate with normal people, like ourselves. Because Branson has shared these wrinkles in himself—and because he has a lot of worthwhile stuff to say—people more easily and readily follow him.

The key to success here is to be authentic. One ill-advised trick that many people try is to pick a weakness that can actually be considered a strength, like saying you are a workaholic. This is the fast path to disaster because business idiots have been trying it for years. No one buys it.

Instead, admit something real. For example, if you are

strong on concepts but weak on double-entry bookkeeping, admit that your assessment should probably be audited. (Unless, of course, you are an auditor, in which case, it's probably better to pick another weakness.)

Another way to show that you are part of the human race is to actually demonstrate that you have some feelings (insert gasp here) about the subject you are addressing. For example, let's say you are talking about offshoring jobs to India or China. Here are two ways to enter that conversation:

The Idiot's Approach: Two hundred and fifty-three of the Global Fortune 500 have moved jobs to Asia in the past three years. To stay competitive, we must seriously consider a similar strategy . . .

The Human Approach: As managers, one of the difficult and sometimes ugly things we have to deal with is taking action that hurts some of our people, but strengthens our company. These issues are never easy to deal with, and I don't have a script for exactly how to think through it . . .

With the human approach, you don't even have to worry about whether people agree with your emotion. By adding a dash of human relevance to your subject, you'll have an audience that really cares.

• • •

You don't need a Ph.D. in psychology to do any of the things we've mentioned here, and those who of us who aren't emotional cretins usually do try to be sensitive to others' concerns. But this approach requires preparation. You need to be sure you really do understand what is on others' minds, or this will just backfire.

These techniques also require loads of confidence. Just

think about your last pitch, presentation, or meeting. How often, and how authentically, did you make the other guy's point? Did you reveal your weaknesses? If you are strong and firm in your conviction, then don't be afraid to venture into the other guy's territory. Because once you are in his territory, it's a lot easier to have a meaningful visit.

14

AN ACTUARY'S GUIDE
TO STORYTELLING

C onsider this. Two books about transformational change. One is a deeply researched work that outlines the eight stages for creating transformational change, written by a renowned professor at Harvard Business School.

Theory vs. Story

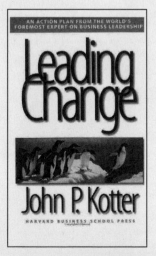 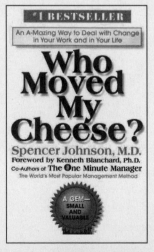

Copies sold: **210,000**
worldwide through 2003

(Source: Harvard Business Review Press.)

Copies Sold: **14 million**
worldwide through 2003

(Source: Putnam.)

Copies sold: 210,000 worldwide. Widely acclaimed, impeccable credentials—and a very strong sales total for a business book.

The second book is a 94-page (AARP font) *story* about a couple of serially dumb rodents wandering around a maze looking for some missing cheese. Copies sold: 14 million worldwide and still going strong. That's a lot of Limburger.

In business, our natural instincts are always left-brained. We create tight arguments and knock the audience into submission with facts, figures, historical graphs, and logic that would do Descartes proud. If the logarithmic scaled charts don't do the trick, we counter with a barrage of bullet points. Tackle them with text boxes. Woo hoo!

The good news is that a lot of what passes as business communications is making a dent in the nation's sleep-deprivation epidemic. The bad news is that the barrage of facts often works against you. My facts against your experiences, emotions, and perceptual filters. Not a fair fight—facts will lose almost every time.

Suppose you're giving an update on customer service levels. You have all the statistics created by the infallible customer relationship management (yes, this is jargon) reporting system your company paid a king's ransom for. Those statistics fill the kind of reports that could do some damage to your foot if they fell off the forklift. But they don't hold a candle to the person in the audience whose husband called the customer service 800 number and ended up waiting longer for a rep than a Cubs fan for a World Series win. The story always trumps a mountain of facts.

Bummer about people—they can just be so *human*.

Of course you know this already. You've heard all of those anthropological accounts of our Neanderthal ancestors huddled around the flickering campfire using narrative to make sense of their world. But, those cave paintings don't do you much good when you're staring down a deadline for that speech or presentation.

The good news is that you don't have to be Sammy the Shaman to spin a good yarn. With a bit of preparation, and a dab of courage, anyone can do this.

THE CAN-THE-DULL-STORY STORY

At just about any sort of business meeting that brings together business idiots who don't work together every day, the meeting starts with introductions. And invariably, most of the crowd says something brilliant like:

> *I'm Billy Blowhard. I'm the Divisional Regional Global Worldwide Operations Manager in charge of everything.*

Who gives a rip?

Next time, when it's your turn, downplay your job and role by at least 75 percent. If you are a product manager, say "My job is to do whatever I can to increase sales for the new and improved Swiffer brooms." If you *are* the CEO and you really are in charge of everything, say something like "I'm so-and-so, and I try to stay out of the way and let people get stuff done." If you're the janitor, it's OK to say something like "I'm the only one with a spotless record in this joint."

Here's the best way to use your title: Write it neatly on a Post-it and stick it in a drawer somewhere. Ditching the title is a fast path off the usual corporate script. It makes people pay attention, because it compels you to tell a story about yourself.

Doesn't sound like a story to you? It's the best kind. By saying very little about yourself, you are actually speaking volumes.

THE "I CAN READ YOUR MIND" STORY

Just think about the last time you were in their shoes. Painful, huh? Just like that—you have a story. By relating your experiences to your audience's concerns, fears, or biases, you have a great story to tell.

You're about to kick off a workshop. You know everyone is worried about having to do one of those cheesy icebreakers, like selecting a toy and then describing how it reminds you of the first time your mother spanked you, or something even more inane.

So, instead of putting everyone through this living hell of pretend cleverness, you tell the group about the stupidest icebreakers you had to do. Better yet, ask people to volunteer their own stories—you get residual credit for their stories.

Or you are about to deliver a sales presentation. You know that your audience is getting pitched to all the time, and the Law of Ginsu Knives always prevails. Everyone hypes the benefits and softens the downside. That's a fact of business life. So you acknowledge it up-front—tell everyone that you know what happens in these types of things and that you get it. Talk about how you hate getting pitched because you are always oversold. Talk about the last time you went shopping for something and the salesman buried you in hype. And you walked out.

All of that misery and idiocy has a silver lining for anyone who can turn it into a story.

Commiseration can be fun.

THE SIMPLE PROP STORY

"If it doesn't fit, you must acquit."

—JOHNNY COCHRANE (O. J. SIMPSON MURDER TRIAL)

That phrase, together with an ill-fitting glove, gave O.J. his walking papers. Mountains of forensic evidence and countless hours of testimony were overshadowed by a simple prop.

© CORBIS SYGMA

• • •

In January 1986, the space shuttle *Challenger* exploded; all seven astronauts aboard were killed. The cause was two simple rubber O-rings. They froze and lost their resiliency; that caused a leak that led to a fire and explosion. Engineers had previously warned of this risk, but they had used technical jargon and obtuse charts, and couldn't convince management of the danger.

At the congressional hearing investigating the disaster, noted physicist Richard Feynman used a very simple prop to make the point. He dropped a tightly clasped O-ring into a glass of ice water. Within moments, the rubber became visibly stiff and inflexible.

© Bettmann/CORBIS

• • •

A high-priced consultant had been working with the CEO of a major company who had an incompetent senior vice president working for him. This senior VP was threatening the health of the entire company. Despite months of counsel and mounds of evidence, the CEO wouldn't act. Finally, the consultant went to the local hardware store and bought a hammer for $12.99. He brought it into the CEO's office, laid it on his desk, and told him that he was figuratively hitting the CEO over the head. He needed to act. Then he left the hammer on his desk as a reminder.

The next week the CEO called the consultant to tell him he had fired the senior VP. He told the consultant that the $12.99 hammer was worth a hell of a lot more than his $350 per hour consulting fees.

• • •

Sometimes, simple props are all you need to tell a memorable story.

THE OUTSOURCE-IT-TO-HOLLYWOOD STORY

What if you could get Steven Spielberg to help you with your presentation? We know that creating great stories can be hard. So why not let the pros do it? A very short movie clip inserted at the right time can be an incredibly powerful way to make your point.

Of course the problem is trying to remember which clip to use in which situation. So we've put together a starter list for you to use in common business situations.

THE BUMPY, GRAINY, TOTALLY UNPROFESSIONAL, CHEAP VIDEO STORY

A team was working with a large retailer on its customer-returns policy. Basically, the problem was that the official policies designed by those know-it-alls at headquarters were being ignored everywhere outside of headquarters. Shocking!

So in doing the review, the team went out to all the stores and found tons of evidence that the policies weren't being followed. Loads of charts and graphs. Enough numbers to torture even Fibonacci. When they made the presentation to management, no one bought it.

So the team bought a cheap video camera and went back out to some of the stores. They filmed interviews with eight sales reps, who cheerily offered up their own versions of the returns policy. These were about as on-target as eight darts thrown by eight blindfolded drunks late at night, but at least the acting was within budget. The bumpy, grainy, totally unprofessional video lasted about four minutes and took less than 5 percent of the time and effort that the rest of the analysis did. And of course it had a profound effect on manage-

HOLLYWOOD OUTSOURCING GUIDE

Theme	Movie Clip *(Time From Start of Movie)*
Don't wait, act now	*Dead Poet's Society* Robin Williams's "Carpe Diem" scene (0:14)
Little things matter a lot	*Any Given Sunday* Al Pacino's locker room scene—game of inches (1:55)
Recognize results above all else	*Jerry Maguire* Tom Cruise's "Show Me the Money!" scene with Cuba Gooding, Jr. (0:28)
Employees aren't motivated	*Animal House* John Belushi's stirring speech to fraternity brothers (1:28)
Don't take the safe route	*Parenthood* Grandma's roller coaster vs. merry-go-round speech to Steve Martin (1:49)
Make the best of the situation	*Apollo 13* NASA engineers throw box of random parts on the table and are told to make it work (1:20)
Anything is possible	*Miracle* Kurt Russell's rousing speech to the U.S. Hockey Team before its match with the Soviets (1:38)
Take a risk— go for it	*Welcome to Mooseport* Gene Hackman "go for the green" speech to Ray Romano (1:26)
The importance of moral integrity	*Mr. Smith Goes to Washington* Jimmy Stewart's filibuster speech just before collapsing on the floor of the Senate (2:01)
Time for a change	*The Odd Couple* Walter Matthau's (Oscar) "I can't take it anymore" rant to Felix (1:30)

ment, who immediately decided to launch a major effort to fix the problems.

The video team didn't even try to be cover everything or nail all the facts. They didn't attempt to present an unbiased case. But seeing is believing. Eight real live people telling simple stories was infinitely more powerful than reams of data.

Some other ways to create your own stories (with or without the camera):

- Visit a store, warehouse, factory, or wherever real work gets done (decidedly *not* the office).
- Call or visit a competitor. Try the product or service.
- Call or visit some customers.
- Visit your distributor's warehouse.
- Flip some burgers—work on the production line.
- Go to some relevant websites and cruise around.
- Call your mom and ask her what she thinks. No one disses moms, because we all understand that mother knows best.

So bring your camera. There's a story waiting to be told.

THE EVERYDAY-LIFE STORY

If you haven't circumnavigated the world in a catamaran you built from scrap plywood, climbed Mt. Everest, or worked in the British Secret Service, you still have a great source for stories. Call on those situations that nearly everyone has experienced. Then build your story from there.

Everyday-life stories start with "Remember when . . ." Everyone has had a first day of school. They felt tense and anxious. They met new friends. Worried about what they were wearing. Checked out their locker. Forgot the combination to their locker. Got lost at least once. Met a really scary teacher. Combed their hair four thousand times.

From there, you tell your story and how it relates to the current situation. If you start with an everyday-life story, you'll immediately establish a connection and rapport with your audience. Unless they were raised by a pack of wolves, they've been there and experienced that. And they can relate to what you are saying.

Some everyday-life examples include:

- Learning to ride a bike
- First date
- First hit in a baseball game
- First pat-down by airport security
- Second pat-down by airport security
- Sneaking a peak at your holiday presents
- Taking your driver's test
- Choosing the wrong line when you're in a hurry
- Creating high jinx in high school
- Being ill and cared for
- Having too much to drink
- Getting rejected by someone
- Getting a pimple
- Losing a loved one
- Finding money on the ground

Basically, life is your canvas. Paint with abandon.

One last piece of advice: Try not to use those everyday-life stories your employer might not condone. You know, like the time you put your boobs on the copying machine to see what kind of job the Canon XD-57 does on them. Stay away from those.

THE "SO WHAT'S THE POINT?" STORIES

In most situations, we usually have a simple message to deliver or point to make. But we also know that we need lots of facts and figures to convince people. After an hour of numbers and statistics, the simple point is usually long forgotten.

One storytelling approach is to identify the essence of what we are trying to say and to construct a story to make the point.

Here's an example from a topic that lots of people are focused on today: Sending work offshore. The typical work about this subject would include lengthy analyses, financial projections, and risk assessments. But the point is simple.

Yes, we could add 100 slides with jagged graphs and vibrant pie charts, but a one-page story about Ricky and Ravi says the same thing. Get to the point, and make it memorable.

THE STUFF-OF-LEGENDS STORIES

Legend has it that sometime in the early 1980s, a man walked into the Fairbanks, Alaska, Nordstrom department store. He carried with him two new snow tires. He went to the first counter he saw, put the tires down, and asked for his money back. Nordstrom, which sells upscale shoes and clothing, has never sold a tire in its history. But that didn't matter. The clerk, living proof of Nordstrom's customer-obsessed culture, reached into the cash register and gave the man $145.

This story has been repeated countless times. It is an incredibly evocative reminder of Nordstrom's customer-centric philosophy. No one knows if the story is true, but that doesn't matter. By drawing on a legendary story, employees and management at Nordstrom are able to powerfully communicate what the company is all about.

A Short Tale about Ricky and Ravi

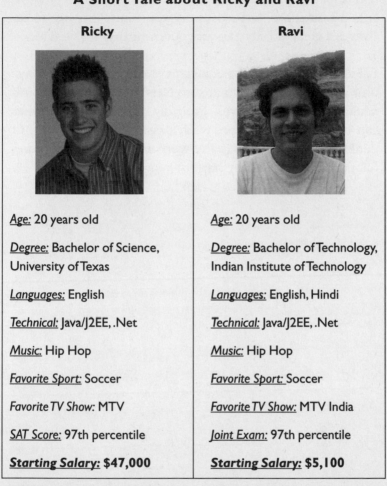

Ricky	Ravi
Age: 20 years old	*Age:* 20 years old
Degree: Bachelor of Science, University of Texas	*Degree:* Bachelor of Technology, Indian Institute of Technology
Languages: English	*Languages:* English, Hindi
Technical: Java/J2EE, .Net	*Technical:* Java/J2EE, .Net
Music: Hip Hop	*Music:* Hip Hop
Favorite Sport: Soccer	*Favorite Sport:* Soccer
Favorite TV Show: MTV	*Favorite TV Show:* MTV India
SAT Score: 97th percentile	*Joint Exam:* 97th percentile
Starting Salary: $47,000	*Starting Salary:* $5,100

Look for stories in your own company. Look in the archives and history of your company. Look for them in your department, and when you find really good ones, get the word out. Find examples of extraordinary customer service. Of how your company cared for employees when they most needed it. Ask for stories about employee feats.

Sometimes, the best new story you can tell to your company is a great old story about your company.

• • •

Storytelling is a fundamental part of being human. We have only a limited capacity to absorb facts, but an enormous capacity to absorb narratives. Probably, this is because stories can be told and conveyed with passion and emotion. Just think about it—emotion in the workplace. If you're not careful, people might actually start listening.

15

THE SUBSTANCE OF STYLE

L et's put the age-old style-vs.-substance debate to bed right away. Consider the case of little Rob and his mom:

"Rob."

"Robby."

"Robby."

"Robert."

"Robberrrtttttt!"

"Robert James Horatio Albert Allen the Third, you little brat, get over here right now!"

With the exception of that last little slip, Rob's mom faithfully used the same content—his name. However, anyone with a mom knows that mothers have as many ways of saying your name as Eskimos have to name snow. And each variation in tone, timbre, and presentation has an entirely different meaning and an entirely different reception by the audience. Just ask little Robby.

So why do we forget that in the business world? Why are we surprised when our amazing content, read with all the breathless excitement of an NPR interview with a cellist, has trouble getting the attention of even a captive audience?

BLAME IT ON DARWIN

Albert Mehrabian, a UCLA professor, conducted a series of famous studies in the early 1970s on the relative importance of different types of communication in conveying meaning. What Mehrabian found was striking: Only 7 percent of the meaning of communications was derived from the words themselves. The other *93 percent* was derived from nonverbal cues—38 percent of the meaning was derived from the way we say things (tonality) and a full 55 percent of the meaning was derived from the physiology of communication, in other words, body language.

The Idiots' Corollary to Mehrabian's study is that the typical business presenter obsesses on that 7 percent—the verbal script. But there's a reason presentation coaches don't want you to deliver everything by rote—that crowds out your personality. You can read your way through a presentation flawlessly, and that won't count for much. The audience was busy noticing the apathy in your voice and the way you avoided looking at your co-presenter—and thinking of the cocktail break coming up in only 6 hours and 47 minutes.

HOW MEANING IS DERIVED

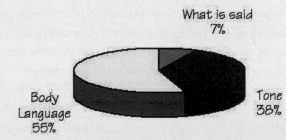

What is said
7%

Body
Language
55%

Tone
38%

We know that people put a lot of stock into what we wear and how we carry ourselves. The entertainment world is full of successful people who get us to pay attention to them, and sometimes even elect them governor of California. In business, this kind of charisma is less common. But these successful people make us care about what they say. We want to know them, look at them, be friends with them. They're comfortable. They're in control. They've mastered that other 93 percent.

How can this be true? Blame it on Darwin. For eons and eons (now there's an estimate we can have some confidence in) we didn't need or have the ability to convey much substance. Neanderthal man's idea of substance was "danger ahead," "water here," "sex now," or "yabba dabba do." Instead, our ancient ancestors became adept translators of style. We have evolved to be exceptionally capable of judging situations and meaning from body language, facial expression, intonation, and the make and model of your car—the *style* side of the substance/style equation. Only very recently have we had to worry about assessing information like manufacturing reports and the capital-asset pricing model.

So the thing to remember is this: Human beings are hard-

"A 1984 study found that *ABC News* anchor Peter Jennings was more likely to smile on camera when talking about Ronald Reagan than Walter Mondale, and that in the same year the people who watched *ABC News* voted for Reagan in greater proportions than the people who watched other network-news shows."

Richard Lacayo, "Spreading the Word." *Time* magazine, Feb 28, 2000, p. 90.

wired to draw much more meaning from *people* than they are from the *information* that people present.

GOOD-LOOKING ON THE RADIO

© *Bettmann/CORBIS*

In 1960, Richard Nixon injured his knee on the way to the studio for the first televised presidential debate with John F. Kennedy. Nixon was not feeling well as a result of the injury, but went forward with the debate. He declined television makeup.

Nixon was no slouch when it came to political sparring. Later research showed that those who listened to the debate on the radio thought Nixon had won.

But the television audience had a vastly different reaction. On television, Nixon was pale and sweating. His shirt collar was loose, and his light gray suit made him fade into the background as if he weren't there. In short, he looked awful.

Kennedy looked like a million bucks. He sported a relaxed tan, and his dark blue suit was crisp and professional. The television audience overwhelmingly supported Kennedy. This debate is widely recognized as a key turning point in the election.

SUITABLY CLUELESS

We recall a particularly awkward session during the height of the dot-com bubble. The Midwest region of a large consulting firm held a staff meeting. The mood was surly. Dot-coms and Internet consultancies were luring away talent with Monopoly-money stock options and free sushi delivered to your cubicle. So the regional manager showed up at a business-casual meeting to address a bunch of twenty-something New Economy wannabees. And he showed up wearing a very *old economy* three-piece Brooks Brothers suit (navy blue, to be precise). Of course, he looked like a complete idiot in front of the audience. It didn't matter what he said. His suit had already delivered the message:

> *Good afternoon, everyone. I'm delighted to announce that I absolutely don't get it.*

Just as voters like their candidates to be presidential in bearing and appearance—smart, confident, and in control—business audiences have expectations, too. CFOs don't like their auditors sporting ponytails any more than CMOs like their advertising creatives wearing wingtips. And young technology experts who want to do big new things in the business world don't want a pep talk from a guy dressed like Woodrow Wilson.

So, that morning trip to the closet actually matters.

VOICE MATCHING: GOODNIGHT MOON

Margaret Wise Brown's enormously popular children's story *Goodnight Moon* has been a part of the bedtime ritual for millions of parents since its publication in 1947. The deceptive beauty of *Goodnight Moon* is that it induces readers to slow down, lower their tone of voice, and use rhythmic patterns. It's not uncommon to find parents sound asleep right next to their toddlers after a reading.

Business people can take a lesson from *Moon*. (No, not the part about putting them to sleep.) Make sure the tone and style of your presentation matches the objective of your communication. *Authentically*. People don't seem to have too much trouble being serious when the time calls for it. It's rare to see a business person flippant about bad earnings, irate customers, or tumbling share prices.

Some situations require the quiet whisper, others the loud boom. It's counterintuitive, but lowering your voice can be a powerful technique to get people to focus. On a practical note, it squelches side conversations and tells people that you're worth some effort to listen to. More important, losing the monotone gives your message emotional weight and makes it more conversational. Your voice is very much the signature of your personality and mood. Don't rubber-stamp your message. Sign it.

It is very common to see business people try to motivate and inspire with a pitch that wouldn't be out of place on one of those miracle dietary supplement infomercials that are always on the air at 2 A.M. (according to what we've heard, anyway). There's nothing worse than a businessperson conveying a false sense of excitement over something mundane, dull, or obviously bad. Like that syrupy confidence in the aftermath of a mediocre product launch.

It sounds idiotic, because it is. People recognize all of the nonverbal cues, and they figure out the truth behind the presentation. The mountain of real clues overwhelms the faked bits and pieces. It could be a bored expression, an occasional glance at the wristwatch, a Freudian slip (everything comes back to Freud, right?), an almost-smile, or a livelier pace. That's the stuff of reality. When the verbal script starts to acquire a kind of barnyard scent, people turn to the other 93 percent of the message.

How many times have you heard an audience evaluate the presentation du jour with comments like these:

He didn't have much enthusiasm.

She didn't seem very excited about what she was saying.

Now think about Martin Luther King Jr.'s famous "I have a dream" speech of 1963. Would he have captured the imagination of white and black Americans alike had he rushed through it like some flight attendant droning on about connecting-gate information? There was a sincerity in his voice that resonated with his words and left no doubt that he meant every word. At times, there was an almost musical quality to his monologue.

Think hard about your demeanor and projection. Do *you* buy what you're saying? How would MLK, or JFK, or Ronald Reagan have said it? (*Would* they have said it?)

There are endless checklists of things to do as a good presenter. Dress appropriately for your audience. Go ahead and get the makeup for television spots. Get voice training before doing a radio broadcast. Get your teeth fixed. (If your boxing career left you with a checkerboard smile, by all means get that distraction fixed.)

There's nothing inherently fake in these ideas. But business idiots think they can substitute these checklists for authenticity, and that's what separates great speakers from idiots with nice makeup.

THE SECRET MAGIC MIRACLE CURE ANSWER

In this book, we haven't had anything good to say about all of those snake oil elixirs and magic potion answers. Because other than the tender words of mom after you've skinned your knee, there are no miracle cures. And there certainly aren't any for business communications.

Well, maybe just one.

And that one, singular, works-every-time answer requires no special instructions, no Anthony Robbins cassettes, no *tai bo* videotapes, and no diet that makes you the biggest watermelon customer in town.

The one thing that you can always rely on is you. *Being you is all you'll ever need.* A lot of people try to be somebody that they're not when they're communicating: the guru, the omniscient executive, the friend of the working class, the cover model for *Fortune*. In any case, the result is usually pretty pathetic.

The answer is not about being someone different—it's about letting more of you out. The real you. The one that laughs, smiles, gets excited when it makes sense to, and shows some emotion. Sometimes it's even OK to get angry. The way to get people to pay attention is to communicate in a manner that connects with their sense of humanity. And that, friends, is the closest thing you'll find to that magic potion.

MONDAY

Got enough guilt to start my own religion.

—TORI AMOS

If it sounds as if we have a lot of firsthand knowledge of jargon, empty hype, fact-free updates, and dull presentations delivered on autopilot, it's because we do. At one time or another, we've made all of the mistakes we've discussed in this book.

All those efforts to follow templates, sugar-coat news, look smart, and deliver polished presentations were supposed to be the ticket to success. But no matter how well we spoke that corporate monotone, it did the opposite of what we wanted. It *stopped* us from getting noticed. We were invisible and silent cogs in the corporate machine. It didn't matter to most people whether one of us delivering the message, or someone else.

Frustrated—and bored with ourselves—we started to bend the rules. We abandoned PowerPoint for props, cut the hard sell and jargon from our e-mails, and used an Eminem song to invite people to an important, very corporate meeting. We told stories instead of summarizing facts. It was nerdy fun, at first, and acceptably naughty, but the effects were real. Fifteen thousand people were actually reading our messages, entering our "Serious Bull" jargon contest, and getting excited about our projects.

Now, when we look back on our careers (and everybody else's), we get it. From the day you enter the corporate world, there's a constant pressure to groom you and make you "normal." That grooming process is supposed to make you a consummate professional, but in reality, it puts a lid on human expression, and if you pop the top of that lid, the blue-suited cartel will suppress you, tell you that you don't fit, or tell you "how things are done around here."

If you've made it this far, you probably don't want to check your soul at the door. If you take anything away from this book, it should be that you don't *have* to check anything at the door but the four traps. There is an amazing opportunity for you to rise above your peers, further your career, sell your ideas, and get what you want just by *being yourself*.

YES, IT'S HARD

It's a little daunting sometimes to stand out, because almost everyone you know is caught in one or two or all four of the traps. It's easier to fall into step and be a templatized clone than it is to put together something honest, witty, or unexpected.

It will take time and courage. When you're sitting there at 11 P.M. on Sunday, preparing an e-mail to your entire team, with your wife and kids tucked safely into bed, your instinct will be to crank out something fast and get it crossed off your list. You won't want to scour the Web for a quote, or question whether your point can be told through a metaphor or a story. You might even succumb to jargon so you don't have to think too hard about whatever it is you're writing. But if you do spend the extra few minutes, and invest some creativity in your communications, you will find a big payoff in how you are received on Monday.

When you're going before those blue suits to ask for budget dollars, you might not feel comfortable deviating from the template, finding an analogy, or going hard on yourself. But this is where you need to take a shot of Red Bull, brush off the naysayers, and give it a try. It's like birth control: choose whatever technique is right for them, and for you.

(OK, so it's not exactly like birth control.)

A SCOUT'S GUIDE TO THE FOUR TRAPS

So there you have it: a whole lot of tips, techniques, and examples. Some of our suggestions will help; some will be irrelevant. You may end up swearing by some of them, and swearing at others.

That's OK. Think of this book as a field guide to the traps—what they are and how you can avoid being transformed into one of the business idiots. Once you recognize the traps, and most important *why* people fall into the traps, you won't be easy prey.

If your heart is set on *informing and not impressing* people, you'll avoid the Obscurity Trap—jargon and evasive language—without trying. If you have a *message in your head that you really care about,* you won't get caught in the Anonymity Trap and settle for some dull, overpolished presentation in the usual anonymous template. If you really have *something valuable to say,* you'll avoid the Hard-Sell Trap and let your audience draw its own conclusion. And if you care enough about your audience to *want to entertain* instead of just getting it over with, your stories will keep you out of the Tedium Trap.

This is a decision to reclaim your voice and commit yourself to connecting with others as a person, not just as a sales manager, technical lead, or (insert your title here). It's fine to admire the corporate stars like Richard Branson and Jeff Bezos, but even better to tap into your own gifts for storytelling, candor, dramatically simple language, pop culture—whatever you do well. It's all the stuff you do on Saturdays when you're with your friends that makes them want to be with you even though there's no agenda. It's not about charts and sales pitches and a bunch of words that you picked out of the thesaurus before you left the office. On the weekend, we take off the corporate mask and speak in a real, compelling voice. And people listen.

Next Monday could be a lot better than last Monday. It could be the first in a long, prosperous, and enjoyable run of Take Your Personality to Work Days.

RESOURCES: A BULL SPOTTER'S GUIDE

Accelerator Fine when referring to a pedal in a car, but bull when used to describe a set of PowerPoint slides or binders that are supposed to reduce a 12-month project to one month's worth of work.

Action item Formerly known as a "task." It's easier to talk about action than to take it, and building "action" into the name makes action even less probable.

Agile Deliberately abstract when applied to business. By fixating on images of gymnasts in tights, you can cause your audience to forget that you've said nothing about how exactly an "agile" 10,000-person corporation remains so limber.

Align Management is an art that desperately wants to be a science. "Organizational alignment" is an especially nebulous form of this bull term.

Architect Why install a new information system when you can "architect the knowledge infrastructure of tomorrow"? Someone ought to tell the business idiots that they're already out-earning almost any architect.

Bandwidth Formerly "time," as in "I don't have the bandwidth to complete any value-added action items." Another case of business assuming a kind of tech savvy that it doesn't have.

Best of breed The whole breeding thing seems to come from a testosterone-driven compulsion to prove that a product has survived some sort of Darwinian natural selection process to become the dominant species. Usually you'll hear this from out-of-shape IT guys who spend a lot of evenings eating french fries at their desk and don't do much in the way of breeding.

Best practice "Practice" connotes respected professions like medicine and law. By calling any slapdash solution a "best practice," business idiots imply that it is the product of a lot of value-added (see below) thought leadership (see below).

Bleeding edge A few minutes after "leading edge" became a dull cliché, someone figured out that there had to be something better.

Blocking and tackling Sports envy has polluted business writing to the point where we would expect federal Superfund money to be made available for cleanup.

Brain dump When business idiots think, it's an event akin to depositing trash or making a lengthy restroom visit.

Buy-in Business studliness is all about making deals. "Agreement" is for wusses.

Capability transfer Forget about telling someone how to do something. When it comes to something as valuable as knowledge capital (see below), it's time to effect capability transfer.

Center of excellence Vortex of incomparable splendor, hub of magnificence, apex of awesomeness, whatever. No one likes anyone who works in any of these.

Change agent Before sports envy took hold, Ian Fleming was the patron saint of business. Much like SMERSH, the murder organization outwitted by Fleming's superspy James Bond, our agents will infiltrate the organization and complete the mission.

Client-focused One of those clichés that make you wonder what businesses were doing the rest of the time.

Close the loop Formerly "tell," but the problem with "tell" is that it is a cumbersome word that's difficult to spell, and also it's subject to varying interpretations. (OK, we tried.)

Core competency Many companies can't manage themselves. This phrase is a good cover for their executives to avoid talking about all of those peripheral incompetencies.

Deck PowerPoint has infected the former art of business presentation so completely that we've gone from "PowerPoint presentation" to "PowerPoint slides" to "slides" to "deck." For laypeople, "deck" is translated as "irrelevant recycled cookie-cutter standard presentation in a can." So, you can see that "deck" is actually shorter.

Deliverable A lot of businesses don't actually make anything. These businesses make "deliverables."

Disintermediate Six syllables that might mean "cut out the middleman." Or they might not. We don't know, and we probably weren't supposed to.

Drill down Go into more detail. Or dig ourselves into a deeper hole. Another symptom of the management art's repressed desire to be a science. Everything comes down to Freud—remember that.

Drink from a fire hydrant A bull term that mercifully died of its own inanity. Which is good, because, no one has the bandwidth to drink from a fire hydrant without getting stressed out from information overload.

Empower Formerly "to delegate," but people figured out that you didn't want a lot of stuff delegated to you.

End to end Something that is soup-to-nuts, enterprise-wide, and seamless is end to end.

Envisioneer Kind of a sophisticated, futuristically brilliant, and imaginatively insightful sort of technical visioning. Kind of.

Extensible Probably "useful for other purposes and in the future," or "not great for any current purpose but possibly useful someday for something."

First mover Formerly "guinea pig," but that term acquired negative connotations at some point. Now recast as a good thing, a "first mover" is a leader in adopting bleeding-edge thoughtware. (See above; see below.)

Frictionless The consulting version of anti-aging cream or the exercise-free fitness program. You should run quickly in the opposite direction when the topic turns to a "frictionless" transition plan, for example.

Full plate Formerly hip expression for "busy," but largely supplanted by the soon-to-be-formerly-hip "no bandwidth," all of which points to the fact that "busy" never really needed replacing.

Future proof See "Frictionless" above.

Game plan If you consider project spreadsheets and timeline charts to be a fun kind of sport, one worthy of live broadcast coverage, "game plan" could be a bull term to add to your vocabulary.

Geopolitical Also geosociopolitical, sociogeopolitical, and sociogeohistopolitical. Best translated as "Because a lot of crap is happening in the real world . . ."

Going forward As in, the "going-forward plan." Easier than whatever the opposite is.

Go-live Captures the intense drama of using a new computer system on Monday. Also says a lot about whoever thinks this is an exciting event.

Guesstimate A guess at an expensive hourly billing rate.

Holistic You might think this means "taking everything into consideration," but it's closer to "based on an incomplete understanding and in the absence of some important data that we wouldn't grasp anyway."

Impactful Formerly "effective," but this implies that you know what you're trying to achieve. "Impactful" promises only that something will happen without committing to anything specific or even positive. One of the more evasive bull terms.

Incentivise Like "incent," but with more syllables, more letters, and a sort of intellectualish aura, kind of.

Infomediary If you know how to align communications channels to create a going-forward value proposition to propel information along the critical path, "infomediary" needs no explanation.

Inoculate As in "inoculate the stakeholders." Less alarming than "defuse the impending outrage," so "inoculate" is a useful bull term for business idiots who have set up permanent residence in the bowels of the Obscurity Trap.

Knowledge base Knowledge.

Knowledge capital Knowledge.

Leading edge See "Bleeding edge." Now a cliché, so in effect something that is "leading edge" is now normal or even outdated, but not "benchmark," which is older than "leading edge" and far older than "bleeding edge." Basically, unless you're shopping for antiques, you'll want "bleeding edge" and should only accept "leading edge" if it's on sale or something.

Leverage Use. Outside of the financial world, "leverage" is idiotspeak intended to assign great value to the thing being used. You might "leverage knowledge capital," instead of "using some old training materials," even if the thing being used is the same.

Mindshare We don't know.

Mission critical The James Bond variant of "critical path," but with the built-in excitement that comes with knowing that what you and many others thought was a stupid project is actually a mission, albeit still a stupid one.

Monetize As in "monetize our extensible competencies," or "monetize the transformational outcomes." You know, "monetize." (Unless you're working in a mint, coining money, this is a great word to never use again.)

Offline "Let's talk about this offline." An aspirational phrase used by idiots who are tired of merely *using* computers and have spiritually become one with their PC.

Off-load Delegate, but obscure enough to make it sound more so-phisticated than just saying that you're weaseling out of a particular bit of work.

Out of pocket Unavailable, but implies a kind of mysterious inaccessibility that leaves open the possibility that you'll be on safari or doing another one of those Mt. Everest jaunts.

Out of the loop A weasel way of saying that someone is an out-of-touch idiot.

Outside the box As in "think out of the box." A last-ditch attempt to get business idiots to think instead of simply forwarding e-mail and re-shuffling PowerPoint presentations.

Paradigm shift Business idiots use this to refer to anything done differently. Darwin's theory of evolution and Copernicus's discovery that the earth revolves around the sun caused paradigm shifts. Outsourcing your company's payroll may be a good idea, but if it was sold as a "paradigm shift," you paid too much.

Parking lot In meetings, a sheet of flipchart paper that contains questions the presenters don't want to answer. The parking lot metaphor would work only if every time you parked your car someone towed it away and sent it to the crusher.

Phase-contain As in "phase-contain the issues log." Really this means "get things done," but business idiots like to phase-contain. For example, new parents often phase-contain toilet training to the toddler phase.

Ping Network technicians ping a network node to confirm that it's functional. Business idiots "ping" everyone, because it makes whatever they actually do sound essential and demanding of real skills.

Productize Probably means "to market," but that wouldn't sound quite as brilliant.

Push the envelope Figuratively, do something better than it has ever been done before. But usually used to describe a competent job at any suitably obscure task. Example: "Doug really pushes the envelope when it comes to delivering value on bleeding edge enterprise transformations."

Quality-driven If you have to say this . . .

Radar screen Another espionage and military term intended to make project management sound like it isn't seriously boring. A euphemism for "don't do anything about this now, but if it turns out to be important later and you forget about it later, you're fired."

Reach out Contact, but reaching out sounds more enlightened, as if you're creating a spiritual bond with the guy who backs up the database instead of simply telling him to back up the database.

Reengineer The most overused term in management consulting, but has also contaminated a lot of formerly normal, well-adjusted technology managers. Once upon a time, "reengineer" meant serious, fundamental change. Now it means installing new software that must be indistinguishable from the old software.

Reinvent the wheel Forget that nothing we've done since the invention of the wheel seems to last for more than a couple of years. Here's a self-congratulatory reference to our ability to complete a 30-day task by finding something left over on our PCs from the last project and spending 32 days to rework it into something useful for the current project.

Repository Another loaded phrase, implying that the place we keep all the stuff that helps us to not reinvent the wheel is seriously organized, and the stuff is like gold bullion.

Repurpose Usually affixed to "knowledge capital" or some other overblown bull term, but really means nothing more than "reuse."

Results-driven The opposite of this is "for the sheer hell of it," but because so few business proposals have succeeded by describing that a project will be done "for the sheer hell of it," this is a good expression to lose.

Scalability May have real meaning, in the sense that an application may serve from one to some very large number of clients, but usually a gratuitous adjective applied to give a technology aura to something vague and worthless. "We offer a scalable value proposition."

Seamless Interfaces are the legendary money pit of technology implementations. "Seamless" is the legendary bit of bull that comes in handy for pre-denial of all those glitches and miscommunications that are one hundred percent likely to occur in any business situation.

Skin in the game It wouldn't be too compelling to begin a business venture by saying that "as long as we're paid, we're not overly concerned about how things turn out." Fortunately, this empty expression allows us to feign concern while remaining not overly concerned about how things turn out.

Socialize As in "socialize the idea." The implication is that we have something better in mind than having the CEO tell everyone they need to adopt the idea or leave. So, often "socializing" includes a carefully crafted memo, using leading-edge communication techniques, telling everyone they need to adopt the idea or leave.

Soup to nuts Complete, but "complete" isn't the kind of word business idiots want to throw around. For one thing, a lot of people know what "complete" means.

Stakeholder Technically, someone who's affected, but if you want to imply that a lot of expensive analysis has been taken to determine—well—who's affected, "stakeholder" could be the right bit of jargon for you.

Strategic A real word but overused to cost-justify a lot of nonstrategic stuff to the point where it has reached the first circle of jargon hell. "Our newest strategic initiative is to replace the call center headphones, some of which are broken."

Synch up Talk or bring up to date, but implies a kind of technical and organizational precision that falls into the category of wishful thinking.

Thought leadership It might sound impossibly arrogant to say that we're smarter than everyone else and are solely qualified to serve as a model for everyone's thought processes regarding a given topic. But apparently it's not impossible.

Thoughtware Formerly "knowledge," but now having been bitten by the technology bug. A lot of business idiots want to understand technology, but in the meantime we have expressions like "thoughtware" that let us project our software envy onto nontechnical stuff that anyone would know having done it once.

Touch base The sports-envy bull term for "tell." The problem with "tell" and "discuss" is they don't sound professional, and too many people will understand what we mean.

Transformation See "Reengineer." "Transformation" has become such a cliché, used for any noticeable change, that we all now assume that switching rental car companies from Avis to Hertz or vice versa is a true business transformation.

Unleash Implies that the intellectual power of whatever we're doing is something the world has never beheld until now. The world is *very* lucky to have us.

Utilize Use, but with the added benefit of more syllables and a more statistical kind of aura to it. (OK, we tried.)

Value add The ultimate marketing hype in a convenient noun. Doesn't say anything, but promises that the result will make something more valuable. Doesn't say what will be more valuable or why, but does promise a positive outcome. Doesn't quantify that outcome, but at least you know you're getting a value add.

Value proposition The reason for doing something, but with an aura of accounting legitimacy without the inconvenience of actual hard numbers or accountants.

Walk the talk Classic management cliché that demonstrates you've read the important management literature from the 1970s.

Win-win Cheerleading, hard-sell, "Kumbaya" bullshit. Otherwise no problems with this charming expression.

World-class Whenever someone has to affix the "world-class" label to anything, rest assured it isn't.

ACKNOWLEDGMENTS

Jon would like to thank:

My niece Elle: my trusted proofreader, ultimate critic, and arbiter of what held water and what didn't. I eagerly await Elle's further reactions to the book in a few months when she turns four.

Ali Kuzu, my Deloitte friend and colleague who burned the midnight oil with me to create the Bullfighter software. No one else could cover an entire conference room wall with algorithms and graphs showing the calculations for how much bull was in a document.

Timothy Clifton, who dragged me to writers' conferences and workshops with the idea that someday I'd have the guts to actually write something, and who read the entire manuscript on dollar-taco night at the local "Mexican" pub, even after the beer was gone.

Jayme McManaway, for taking a leave of absence to teach in Spain, and taking those bullfight photos that wound up being used as much more than souvenirs.

Addison Eisenbarth-DeBolt, Ryan Hartman, and Bud Minton of Deloitte—the creative force in San Francisco that made our Bullfighter software look great.

Chelsea would like to thank:

My Dad, a man of enormous warmth, wit, and good will, who gave me so many gifts, including a love of language and an appreciation for the written word. He was the single greatest supporter of this book, and of me. He is profoundly missed and affectionately remembered, each and every day.

My Mom, who planted the seed of this crusade by taking her four-month-old to a national convention of English teachers fuming about public doublespeak. She then imprinted the cause on my psyche by toting a bag burnished with the word "BULLSHIT" throughout my formative years.

My personal Board of Directors: Yana, Pard, Chev, Wurz, and Beau, and all of my wildly supportive friends. You never flinched when I launched my laptop at the local pub or feverishly scribbled napkin notes over dinner. And you read every draft and approached every title flip-flop with renewed interest and support.

Geoff, the kind soul from the Genius Bar at the Apple store in SoHo, whose superhuman heroics in the face of The Chianti Catastrophe rescued our final manuscript from the doom that befell the rest of my computer.

Brian would like to thank:

First and foremost, my wife, Gail, who graciously accepted the fact that we would be the only family in the neighborhood where bovine excrement was a regularly featured topic at the dinner table.

My children, Kevin, Lisa, Kelsey, and Scottie, who have taught me that there is absolutely no point in being grown up if you can't be childish sometimes.

My friends Dan Gruber, Bill Vaculin, and Scott Whitmer, who gave us tons of great ideas, 99 percent of which we totally ignored.

My friend and colleague Jack Witlin, perhaps the least articulate—and most effective—communicator I've ever known.

All the neighbors, friends, and unknown strangers in pizza joints, planes, and bars, who politely participated in a never-ending series of spontaneous focus groups (and none of whom agreed on a damn thing).

My colleagues at Deloitte, who were willing (usually) guinea pigs in our sometimes weird and bizarre communications experiments.

We all would like to thank:

The greatest bull spotter of all time, Linda Graf, who saved our asses more times than we can count.

The picadors at Free Press, who helped us put our rants and wisdom into print: our editor Fred Hills, publisher Suzanne Donahue, publicist Elizabeth Keenan, and editorial assistant Kirsa Rein.

Our agent, Jim Levine, who spanked us when we needed it.

Our colleague Jason English, the master researcher behind the Starbucks study and a straight-talking guy who can nonetheless lay claim to being one of the world's foremost authorities on bullshit.

Our friends at C2, who consistently proved to us, despite our predictable complaints, that thinking wrong is always right. They have been enormously helpful in shaping our ideas (including the really weird stuff).

Lana Rigsby from Rigsby Design, for mercifully liberating us from our own self-imposed hell brought on by The Great Cover Debate.

ABOUT THE AUTHORS

Brian Fugere is a recovering jargonaholic. After authoring some of the worst jargon the consulting world has ever seen, he formally admitted his problem and entered a twelve-step program. He is currently in rehab and has been clean for the last two years. He is a principal of Deloitte Consulting LLP, where he was formerly Chief Marketing Officer. Brian lives in Danville, California, with his wife, Gail, and their four children.

Chelsea Hardaway is an authenticity nut. She can detect hogwash and spin from a country mile, and has spent her career helping companies trade in the usual corporate gibberish for more honest, human communications. She is the president of Hardaway Productions, a brand and communications consultancy that helps clients cut through the clutter. Previously, she was the global brand director at Deloitte Consulting LLP. Chelsea lives in Montara, California.

Former eighth grade spelling champion **Jon Warshawsky** is a manager at Deloitte Services LLP and helped start the firm's e-Learning practice. In 2000, he founded *Cappuccino,* a newsletter covering organizational change and learning. In 2002, Mr. Warshawsky returned to his roots as a grammar curmudgeon and led the development of Bullfighter, the software that quantified idiocy in the world of business writing. He lives in San Diego.